1 MONTH OF
FREE
READING

at
www.ForgottenBooks.com

By purchasing this book you are eligible for one month membership to ForgottenBooks.com, giving you unlimited access to our entire collection of over 1,000,000 titles via our web site and mobile apps.

To claim your free month visit:
www.forgottenbooks.com/free1327845

ISBN 978-0-428-89110-7
PIBN 11327845

For support please visit www.forgottenbooks.com

CALENDAR

OF

Queen's University and College,

KINGSTON, CANADA.

SESSION 1863-64.

INCORPORATED BY ROYAL CHARTER.

KINGSTON:
PRINTED FOR THE UNIVERSITY BY JOHN ROWLANDS.

1863.

Queen's University and College, Kingston.

PRINCIPAL—VERY REV. WILLIAM LEITCH, D.D.

FACULTIES OF THEOLOGY AND ARTS.

THE PRINCIPAL,
Primarius Professor of Divinity.

Rev. JOHN B. MOWAT, M.A.,
Professor of Oriental Languages, Biblical Criticism and Church History.

Rev. JAMES WILLIAMSON, LL.D.,
Professor of Mathematics and Natural Philosophy.

Rev. GEORGE WEIR, M.A.,
Professor of Classical Literature, and Secretary to the Senatus.

GEORGE LAWSON, Ph. D., LL.D.,
Professor of Natural History.

Rev. JOHN C. MURRAY,
Professor of Logic and Mental and Moral Philosophy, and Registrar.

FACULTY OF MEDICINE.

THE PRINCIPAL,
President of the Medical Faculty.

JOHN R. DICKSON, M.D.,
Professor of the Principles and Practice of Surgery, Dean of the Medical Faculty.

HORATIO YATES, M.D.,
Professor of the Principles and Practice of Medicine.

FIFE FOWLER, M.D., L.R.C.S., Edinburgh,
Professor of Materia Medica and Pharmacy.

J. P. LITCHFIELD, M.D.,
Professor of Forensic and State Medicine.

GEORGE LAWSON, Ph. D., LL.D.,
Professor of Chemistry and Practical Chemistry, Secretary to the Faculty.

M. LAVELL, M.D.,
Professor of Obstetrics and Diseases of Women and Children.

RODERICK KENNEDY, M.D., L.R.C.S., Edinburgh,
Professor of Anatomy.

OCTAVIUS YATES, M.D.,
Professor of the Institutes of Medicine.

MICHAEL SULLIVAN, M.D.,
Demonstrator in Anatomy.

FACULTY OF LAW.

HONORABLE ALEXANDER CAMPBELL, Speaker of the Legislative Council,
Dean of the Faculty of Law.

JAMES ALEX. HENDERSON, Esq., D.C.L., Master in Chancery,
Professor.

GEORGE W. DRAPER, Esq., M.A.,
Professor.

All official communications regarding general University matters should be addressed to the Registrar, Professor MURRAY.

BENEFACTIONS.

Colonial Committee, Church of Scotland, Annual Grant, £300 stg., in aid of the Faculty of Theology	$1460 00
Colonial Committee, Church of Scotland, Annual Grant for Scholarship or Bursary Fund, £50 stg.	243 33
Endowment of Ladies' Association, Toronto, for Annual Scholarship or Bursary	800 00
Endowment of Ladies Association, Kingston, for Annual Scholarship or Bursary	1113 00
Donation, His Royal Highness the PRINCE OF WALES, invested as a Prize Fund	800 00
Bequest of the late JOHN MOWAT, Esq., for endowment of an Annual Competition Scholarship	800 00
Annual Grant for Scholarship from HUGH ALLAN, Esq., Montreal	50 00
Scholarship by Hon. ALEX. CAMPBELL	80 00
Scholarship by JOHN WATKINS, Esq.	80 00

Scholarships, varying in annual value, from :

> Montreal Lay Association, three annually.
> St. Andrew's Church, Hamilton.
> St. Andrew's Church, Montreal.
> Missionary Association of St. Andrew's University.
> Missionary Association of Aberdeen University.
> Missionary Association of Glasgow University.
> Contributions from Congregations and Associations for Bursary Fund.

Donations of Books from :

ALEX. MORRIS, Esq., M.P.P.	30 vols.
Tract Society, London	134 "
Principal LEITCH	87 "
Mrs. JOHN MOWAT	26 "
President NELLES	19 "
United States Patent Office	9 "
Rev. Professor STEVENSON, Edinburgh	7 "
J. J. BURROWES, Esq.	7 "
Provincial Government	10 "
Smithsonian Institution, Washington	20 "
Geological Survey of Canada	8 "
Dr. SAMPSON	30 "
Botanical Society of Edinburgh	5 "
Rev. R. V. ROGERS	38 "
Swedenborg Association, per DAVID GILMOUR, Esq., Paisley, Scotland	27 "
ANDREW DRUMMOND, Esq.	14 "

6

A. T. DRUMMOND, Esq., B.A., LL.B., and Fellow of
    Queen's University ... ... 14 vols.
JOHN CREIGHTON, Esq. ... ... 12 "
Professor MURRAY ... ... "
Association for the Promotion of Social Science ... ... "
Regents of the University of the State of New York ... "
R. J. DRUMMOND, Esq. ... ... "
Professor WILLIAMSON ... ... "
R. H. PATTERSON, Esq. ... ... "
JUDGE LOGIE, ... "
Single Volumes from various parties ... ... "

Donation of Reflecting Telescope to Observatory by Principal LEITCH.

Donation of Achromatic Telescope to Observatory, by ARCHIBALD JOHN MACDONELL, Esq.

Donation of extensive collections of Fossils and Minerals from the Geological Survey, by Sir WILLIAM LOGAN, Director.

Donation of a large collection of Canadian Fossils and Minerals, chiefly Canadian, from Professor WILLIAMSON.

Bequest of Rev. Andrew BELL, of Canadian Fossils and Minerals.

Donations of Specimens from Rev. R. CAMPBELL, Mr. FOX, Mr. OLIVER, Mr. HARKNESS, Mr. ALEX. BELL, Mr. COWAN, &c.

CALENDAR FOR 1863–4.

	SUNDAY.	MONDAY.	TUESDAY.	WEDNESDAY.	THURSDAY.	FRIDAY.	SATURDAY.
OCTOBER...					1	2	3
	4	5	6	7	8	9	10
	11	12	13	14	15	16	17
	18	19	20	21	22	23	24
	25	26	27	28	29	30	31
NOVEMBER.	1	2	3	4	5	6	7
	8	9	10	11	12	13	14
	15	16	17	18	19	20	21
	22	23	24	25	26	27	28
	29	30					
DECEMBER.			1	2	3	4	5
	6	7	8	9	10	11	12
	13	14	15	16	17	18	19
	20	21	22	23	24	25	26
	27	28	29	30	31		
JANUARY ..						1	2
	3	4	5	6	7	8	9
	10	11	12	13	14	15	16
	17	18	19	20	21	22	23
	24	25	26	27	28	29	30
	31						
FEBRUARY.		1	2	3	4	5	6
	7	8	9	10	11	12	13
	14	15	16	17	18	19	20
	21	22	23	24	25	26	27
	28	29					
MARCH....			1	2	3	4	5
	6	7	8	9	10	11	12
	13	14	15	16	17	18	19
	20	21	22	23	24	25	26
	27	28	29	30	31		
APRIL.....						1	2
	3	4	5	6	7	8	9
	10	11	12	13	14	15	16
	17	18	19	20	21	22	23
	24	25	26	27	28	29	30

ACADEMIC YEAR 1863-64.

1863.	
June 25	Competitive Examination for Scholarships in College Grammar School.
" 26	Grammar School Examinations—Spring Term ends.
July 3.	Meeting of Board of Visitors of the Observatory.
Aug. 10	Grammar School Summer Term begins.
Octob. 7	Opening of the University Session by Public Address in Convocation Hall at 3 o'clock. Session of the Faculty of Arts opens. Session of the Faculty of Medicine opens.
" 8	Matriculation Examinations in Faculty of Arts commence. Competitive Examinations for Mowat Scholarship.
" 9	First Meeting for the Session of Botanical Society, at Eight o'clock, P.M.
Nov'r 2	No Lectures in Arts.
" 4	Theological Classes open.
" 13	Botanical Society meets at 8 o'clock P.M.
Dec'r 7	No Lectures in Theology and Arts.
" 11	Botanical Society meets at 8 o'clock P.M.
" 22	Grammar School Examinations—Autumn Term ends.
" 24	First day of Christmas Vacation in all the Faculties of the University, and in the Grammar School.
1864. Jan'y 1	Meeting of Board of Visitors of the Observatory.
" 4	Session of Law Faculty opens.
" 6	Classes resumed in all the Faculties after Christmas Vacation. Lectures in the Law Faculty are discontinued during the Sittings of the Quarter Sessions.
" 7	Grammar School Winter Term begins.
" 8	Meeting of Senate to elect a Hospital Governor and Curators of the Library. Botanical Society meets at 8 o'clock P.M.
Jan'y 31	Two Grammar School Trustees to retire, their successors to be elected by the County Council at their first meeting after 1st January.

Feb'y	1	No Lectures in Theology and Arts.
"	3	Meeting of Grammar School Trustees.
"	12	Botanical Society meets at 8 o'clock P.M.
"	19	Class Tickets, Certificates of Attendance, &c., to be given in by Students of Medicine who intend to present themselves either at the Primary or at the Final Examination.
		Theses to be given in by intending Graduates in Medicine.
"	26	First Public Lecture on Astronomy in the City Hall.
March	4	Regular Lectures in Medical Faculty concluded.
		Second Public Lecture on Astronomy in the City Hall.
"	7	No Lectures in Theology and Arts.
"	9	Extra Professional, Primary and Final Examinations in Medical Faculty commence, continued on succeeding days.
"	11	Botanical Society meets at 8 o'clock P.M.
"	29	Public Defence of Theses in Medical Faculty at 10 o'clock, afterwards Meeting of Senate to decide as to the granting of Degrees.
"	30	Classes in Law Faculty close. Grammar School Spring Term begins.
"	31	Meeting of Convocation, for laureation of Medical Graduates, at 3 o'clock P.M.
April	1	Theses for M.A. given in.
"	4	No Lectures in Theology and Arts.
"	8	Botanical Society meets at 8 o'clock P.M.
"	9	Examination in Law Faculty for Degree of LL.B.
"	15	Regular Class work of Theological and Arts Classes concluded.
"	18	Written Examination of Junior Class in Classics. Written examination of second year's Class in Mathematics and Natural Philosophy. Written Examination in Logic and Mental and Moral Philosophy of third year's Class for Degree of B.A. Written Examination in Hebrew, Church History, &c.
"	19	Written Examination of Junior Mathematical Class. Written Examination of second year's Class in Classics.
"	20	Written Examination of third year's Class in Classics for Degree of B.A. Written Examination in Natural History (second year's Class.)

2

April 21	Written Examination in Systematic Theology.
" 21	Written Examination in Mathematics and Natural Philosophy for B.A.
	Written Examination on first year's extra subjects.
	Written Examination on second year's extra subjects.
" 22	Written Examination on third year's extra subjects.
	Oral Examination of Junior Classes.
" 23	Oral Examination of second year's Classes.
" 25	Oral Examination of third year's Classes for Degree of B.A.
" 26	Defence of Theses in Arts at 10 o'clock.
	College Senate meets to decide on passing of Candidates for Degrees in Theology, Law and Arts.
" 28	Meeting of Convocation, for laureation of Graduates in Theology, Law and Arts, for the distribution of Prizes and for the election of Fellows.

TIME TABLE OF THE MEETING OF CLASSES, &c.

HOURS.	FACULTY OF ARTS.	FACULTY OF LAW.	FACULTY OF THEOLOGY.		FACULTY OF MEDICINE.	
8—9 A.M	Prayers at 8.45.				Anatomical Demonstrations.	Dissecting Room open from 8 A.M all day.
9—10.	Mathematics, 1st Class. / Classics, 2nd and 3rd Classes.	Law Lectures.	Junior Hebrew.		Materia Medica.	Laboratory open from 9 to 2.
10—11.	Mathematics, 2nd Class. / Classics, 1st Class. / Moral Philosophy and Logic.		Third Hebrew.	Chaldee on Monday.	Chemistry.	
11—12.	Natural Philosophy, 2nd Class. / Classics, 1st Class. / Natural History, 2nd Class.		Divinity.			Institutes of Medicine.
12—1.	Natural Philosophy, 1st Class. / Classics, 1st Class.				Forensic and State Medicine, Tuesdays & Fridays. Hospital, Mondays, Wedn'days and Saturdays.	Practical Chemistry on Mondays, Wednesdays, Thursdays
1—2.	Nat. His., 1st Class, Tuesdays & Fridays					Clinical Medicine on Saturdays.
2—3.	Library open from 2 to half-past 2.		Syriac on Monday.	Arabic on Thursday.	Anatomy.	Clinical Surgery on Saturdays.
3—4.	Moral Philosophy and Logic.		Divinity.			Theory and Practice of Medicine.
4—5.			Church Hist. Mon., Thur.	Bibl'l Criticism, Tues. Wed. Frid.	Surgery.	
5—6.			2nd Hebrew.		Obstetrics.	
6—7.						

None of the Classes meet on Saturdays except those specially mentioned in the above Table as meeting on that day. In the Faculties of Theology and Arts there are no Classes on the first Monday of the month, which is occupied in preparation for the Monthly Examinations.

GENERAL ANNOUNCEMENT.

Candidates for matriculation in the Faculty of Arts as regular Students of the first year will undergo an examination in Greek Grammar; Xenophon, Anabasis, B. I.; Latin Prose Composition; Sallust, Catilina; Caesar, B. I.; Virgil, Æneid, B. I. and II.; Arithmetic, as far as Vulgar and Decimal Fractions, and the Extraction of Roots inclusive, Algebra to the end of Simple Equations; Euclid, B. I., II.

GENERAL ANNOUNCEMENT.

The Session 1863-4 will commence on 7th October, 1863, when the Matriculation Books will be opened by the Secretaries for receiving the names of under-graduates and other students in the various Faculties. The Session will terminate on the last Thursday (the 28th) of April, being the day fixed for graduation in the Faculty of Arts. The staff of Professors in this University is now more complete than it has ever been heretofore; and all the Faculties of Theology, Law, Medicine, and Arts, are in full operation, providing a thorough course of instruction in the various departments, leading to the Degrees in Theology, of B.D.; in Law, of LL.B.; in Medicine, of M.D.; and in Arts, of B.A. and M.A.

In the Faculty of Arts the curriculum extends over three Sessions of seven months each. All Entrants and regular Students in that Faculty are required to be present at the opening of the Session, on the first Wednesday (the 7th) of October. The Medical Session commences on the same day. The Divinity Classes will be opened on the first Wednesday (the 4th) of November; and the Law Faculty will commence their course of instruction on 4th January, 1864. Addresses will be delivered at the opening of the College on 7th October, at 3 o'clock, when all Students are expected to be present. All Students are required, after matriculation in their several Faculties, to wait upon the Registrar and intimate to him the various classes which they are attending each Session.

Candidates for matriculation in the Faculty of Arts as regular Students of the first year will undergo an examination in Greek Grammar; Xenophon, Anabasis, B. I.; Latin Prose Composition; Sallust, Catilina; Cæsar, B. I.; Virgil, Æneid, B. I. and II.; Arithmetic, as far as Vulgar and Decimal Fractions, and the Extraction of Roots inclusive, Algebra to the end of Simple Equations; Euclid, B. I., II.

FEES.

Matriculation, annually	$ 4 00
First year's Classes	32 00
Second year's Classes (including apparatus, $4)	40 00
Third year's Classes (including apparatus, $4)	36 00
A single Class, each hour	8 00
Natural History Class excepted, which is ...	12 00

Students preparing for the Church of Scotland in Canada are exempted from the payment of fees, but if they change their intention of entering the Church, they are bound to pay up the fees remitted.

Each Student on entering must produce a certificate of moral and religious character from the Minister of the Congregation to which he belongs.

The course of study to be pursued, and other requirements for a Degree, are fully detailed in the announcements of the different Faculties. Students who do not desire to proceed to a Degree may enter any Class or Classes in any of the Faculties by simply paying the fee for the Class or Classes desired; but in the Department of Arts no one can rank as an Undergraduate without submitting to the regular matriculation examinations.

Prayers in the Convocation Hall every week day (except Saturday) at a quarter before 9 o'clock A.M., and on Sabbath at a quarter before 10 o'clock.

I.

OPEN SCHOLARSHIPS.

These Scholarships are open to all Students in Arts.

KINGSTON SCHOLARSHIP.

Founded by the Ladies of Kingston and from the proceeds of Lectures by the Professors. Open to all Students of the second year. The University examination at the close of the second year to be the competitive examination. Value, £20. Tenable during the third year of the course. Awarded by the Senatus.

MOWAT SCHOLARSHIP.

Founded by the late JOHN MOWAT, Esq., Kingston. Open to all Students of the first year. Competitive examination on Arithmetic on the 8th of October first year. Value, the interest of £200. Tenable during the first year of the course.

FOUNDATION SCHOLARSHIP.

Open to all Students of the first year. The University examination at the close of the first year to be the competitive examination. Value, £10. Tenable during the second year of the course.

FOUNDATION SCHOLARSHIP.

Open to all Students of the second year. The University examination at the close of the second year to be the competitive examination. Value, £5. Tenable during the third year of the course.

II.

GRAMMAR SCHOOL SCHOLARSHIPS.

CAMPBELL SCHOLARSHIP.

Founded by Hon. ALEX. CAMPBELL. Open to all pupils of the Grammar Schools of Newburgh, Bath, and Kingston, in rotation. The first Scholar to be from Newburgh, for Session 1862-3. The matriculation subjects of Queen's College to be the subjects of competition. Value, £20. Tenable for the first year of the course in Queen's College. When there is no qualified competitor in the Grammar School, the Scholarship will be competed for at the matriculation examination, and be open to all Students of the first year. Preference to be given to a Student of the name of CAMPBELL.

WATKINS SCHOLARSHIP.

Founded by JOHN WATKINS, Esq. Open to all pupils of the College Grammar School. The subjects of the matriculation examination to be those of the competitive examination. Value, £20. Tenable for the first year of the course in Queen's College. To be competed for on the day previous to the public Grammar School examination on the last Friday in June.

QUEEN'S SCHOLARSHIPS.

Open to all the pupils of the College Grammar School. The subjects of the matriculation to be those of the competitive examination. There are three Scholarships, of the value of £10 each. Tenable for the first year of the course at Queen's College. To be competed for on the day previous to the public Grammar School examination on the last Friday of June.

III.

CHURCH SCHOLARSHIPS.

These Scholarships can be held only by Students preparing for the Church of Scotland in Canada, and they must be repaid if the Student change his intention of entering the Church.

TORONTO SCHOLARSHIP.

Founded by the Ladies' Association of Toronto. Open to Students of the first year in Arts. The University examination at the close of the Session to be the competitive examination. Value, £14. Tenable during the second year of the course.

ALLAN SCHOLARSHIP.

Founded by HUGH ALLAN, Esq., for a Student in Divinity. Open to Students of the third year in Arts. The University examination at the close of the Session to be the competitive examination. Value, £12 10s. Tenable during the first year in the Divinity Hall.

ST. ANDREW'S (HAMILTON) SCHOLARSHIP.

Founded by St. Andrew's Church, Hamilton. Open to Students of the second year in the Hall. Competitive examination at the close of the Session on the subjects of the Theological course during the Session. Value, about £10. Tenable during the third year of the course.

MONTREAL SCHOLARSHIPS.

There are three, founded by the Lay Association of Montreal. There is one open to the Students of each year of the Arts course. The University examination at the close of the respective Sessions to be the competitive examination. Tenable respectively for the second and third year in Arts, and the first year in Theology. Value of each about £10.

GLASGOW SCHOLARSHIP.

Founded by the Missionary Society of Glasgow College. Open to Students of the first year in Arts. University examination at the close of the Session to be the competitive examination. Tenable for the second year in Arts. Value, about £10.

ABERDEEN SCHOLARSHIP.

Founded by the Missionary Society of College of Aberdeen. Open to Students of the second year in Arts. University examination at the close of the Session to be the competitive examination. Tenable during the third year in the Arts course. Value, about £10.

ST. ANDREW'S (SCOTLAND) SCHOLARSHIP.

Founded by the Students' Missionary Society. Open to Students of the third year in Arts. University examination at the close of the Session to be the competitive examination. Tenable for the first year in the Divinity Hall. Value, about £10.

ST. ANDREW'S (MONTREAL) SCHOLARSHIP.

Founded by St. Andrew's Church, Montreal. Open to Students of the first year in the Hall. Competitive examination at the close of the Session on the subjects of the Theological course during the Session. Value, about £10. Tenable during the second year of the course.

No Student can hold more than one Scholarship.

IV.

BURSARIES.

Bursaries are held by Students preparing for the Church of Scotland. They are tenable by Students in Theology or Arts. The sum is proportioned to the circumstances of the Student. He is bound to repay the money to the College should he change his intention of entering the Church. No Student can hold a Bursary who is not able to pass the regular University examinations.

LIBRARY.

The Library is open to all Students who have paid a Matriculation Fee in any of the Faculties. A catalogue of the Books has been prepared, copies of which may be obtained from the Librarian, price 10 cents.

During Session the Library is open daily at two o'clock and continues open for at least half an hour after that time, for giving out and receiving Books. During the summer recess it is open from 9 to 10 A.M. on Saturdays only.

For convenience of consultation, a portion of the Books will be kept at the Medical Buildings and at the Observatory.

ASTRONOMICAL OBSERVATORY.

The Kingston Observatory was founded in 1855 by private subscribers, aided by the Corporation and citizens of Kingston, and transferred by deed of the Corporation in 1861 to the University. It contains an Equatorial by Mr. ALVAN CLARKE, with an object-glass of 6¼ inches aperture, a Reflecting Telescope by the celebrated Mr. SHORT, with a speculum of 7½ inches in diameter, presented by the Principal, and a Refracting Telescope, presented by A. J. MACDONELL, Esq. A new building was erected by the College in 1861, containing, besides the central dome for the Equatorial, a Transit Room, and room for the Observers and the public. The Transit Room will soon be furnished with a Transit and Clock. A course of not less than six lectures on Astronomy, open to the public, is delivered each year in the City Hall and the Observatory.

MUSEUM.

The Museum at present consists chiefly of Mineralogical and Palæontological specimens. It embraces the collections of Canadian Minerals and Fossils bequeathed by the late Rev. A. BELL, together with the collections made by the Rev. Prof. WILLIAMSON, and contributions, illustrating very fully the Minerals and Fossils of Canadian Rocks, presented by Sir WILLIAM LOGAN, Director of the Geological Survey. Admission to the Museum may be obtained by applying to the Professor of Natural History or to the Janitor of the College. Occasional demonstrations are given to Students.

DONATIONS TO MUSEUM.

From Mrs. McLEOD, Johnson Street, Kingston, specimen, preserved in alcohol, of the Flower of the Great Night Flowering Cactus (Cereus grandiflorus).

From Rev. ROBERT BURNET, Hamilton, a very fine Bear's Skull.

From JOHN PATON, Esq., Kingston, an interesting series of Minerals, including Galena or Sulphide of Lead from Thunder Bay, Magnetic Iron Ores from the north shore of Lake Superior, beautiful violet colored Quartz Crystals, native Copper, and also Carbonates and Sulphides of Copper from the Bruce Mines, with various samples of the ore crushed and separated from the quartz, &c., by washing.

From Dr. GRANT, Ottawa, specimen of Fungus used as a remedy in Rheumatism (referred to in Dr. GRANT's Paper in Brit. Amer. Jour. of Medicine, 1862).

From Mr. Thomas F. Harkness, B.A., specimen of the same.

From Mr. Alexander Bell, Perth, specimen of Michelinia convexa, a fossil of the Corniferous Limestone, Magnetic Iron Ore from the line of the Brockville Railway, fine crystals of Apatite (phosphate of lime), and various other Minerals, Indian Implements, &c.

From Mr. John Bell, B.A., a remarkably fine specimen of Graphite from Argenteuil.

From the Very Rev. Principal Leitch, D.D., Skin of the Ptarmigan or "White Partridge" (Lagopus vulgaris).

From Mr. Edward C. Fox, Skins of several Canadian Birds.

From Mr. Robert V. Rogers, B.A., a collection of Canadian Insects.

STATEMENT OF THE NUMBER OF SPECIMENS IN THE BELL COLLECTION IN QUEEN'S COLLEGE MUSEUM.

The whole of the specimens contained in the "Bell Collection" (bequeathed by the late Rev. Andrew Bell, of L'Orignal) have been carefully gone over, re-labelled, and the arrangement to some extent revised, by Mr. Robert Bell, Jr., of the Provincial Geological Survey. The following is a statement of the number of specimens which the collection contained, January, 1863 :—

I.	Minerals and specimens of Metamorphic Rocks	672
II.	Potsdam and Calciferous Formations	191
III.	Chazy Formation	52
IV.	Trenton Group	427
V.	Utica Formation	119
VI.	Hudson River do.	173
VII.	Medina do.	57
VIII.	Clinton and Niagara Formations	530
IX.	Guelph Formation	181
X.	Onondaga do.	46
XI.	Oriskany do.	40
XII.	Corniferous do.	195
XIII.	Hamilton do.	56
XIV.	Species of Mollusca, and miscellaneous specimens illustrative of the Superficial Geology of Canada	99
XV.	Indian Antiquities	195
XVI.	Miscellaneous	7
	Total number of specimens	3040

BOTANICAL SOCIETY.

The meetings of the Botanical Society of Canada are usually held in the Convocation Hall of the College, on the evenings of the second Friday of the month during session.

The Botanic Garden contains an accurately named and labelled collection of hardy plants; including most of the economical, medicinal, and poisonous plants of Europe and America, capable of being grown in the open air at Kingston. The plants are being arranged in natural orders for convenience of study, and the Botanical Class receives daily demonstrations in the open air during the early part of the session.

The Society's Herbarium, to which Students have access on Saturdays, embraces extensive collections of native plants from various parts of Canada. It includes the collections made by the Officers of the Geological Survey, which were placed by the Director, Sir WILLIAM LOGAN, under the Society's charge.

DONATIONS.

From Harvard University, Cambridge, Mass., per Prof. ASA GRAY, a large collection of Plants for the Botanic Garden.

From JOHN WATKINS, Esq. $100 00
From JOHN CARRUTHERS, Esq. 50 00

Donations to the Garden, Herbarium, and Library, from Judge LOGIE; HUGH FRASER, Esq.; G. BAXTER, Esq.; THOS. BRIGGS, Esq.; Miss MASON; Prof. CARUEL, Florence; Dr. MULLER, Melbourne; Prof. FOWLER; Prof. LITCHFIELD; Prof. WILLIAMSON; M. FLANAGAN, Esq.; A. DRUMMOND, Esq.; B. BILLINGS, Jr., Esq.; Mr. J. MACOUN; Principal DAWSON; T. BOG, Esq.; G. S. HOBART, Esq.

FACULTY OF ARTS.

The Very Rev. WILLIAM LEITCH, D.D., Principal and Primarius Professor.

CLASSICS.

Rev. GEORGE WEIR, M.A., Professor.

First Year.

CLASS BOOKS.

1. Homer, Iliad, B. VI.
2. Lucian, Vita et Charon.
3. Greek Prose Composition.

1. Cicero, De Amicitia.
2. Virgil, Æneid, B. VI.
3. Horace, Odes, B. I.
4. Latin Prosody.
5. Roman Antiquities.
6. Latin Prose Composition.

Second Year.

CLASS BOOKS.

1. Demosthenes, Philippics.
2. Euripides, Alcestis.
3. Greek Prosody and Prose Composition.
4. Greek Antiquities.

1. Cicero, pro Milone.
2. Horace, Epodes.
3. Virgil, Georg. IV.
4. Latin Prose Composition.

Third Year.

CLASS BOOKS.

1. Plato, Apology and Crito.
2. Sophocles Œdipus Coloneus.
3. Greek Composition.
4. Arnold's Greek and Roman Antiquities.

1. Tacitus, Annals, B. I.
2. Livy, B. XXI.
3. Latin Composition.
4. Terence, Phormio.

Additional for honors.
5. Æschylus, Prometheus Vinctus.

MATHEMATICS AND NATURAL PHILOSOPHY.

Rev. JAMES WILLIAMSON, M.A., LL.D., Professor.

First Year.

CLASS BOOKS.

1. Euclid, B. I., II., III., IV., V., and VI., (Simson, small edition.)
2. Algebra (Wood's or Hind's).
3. Plane Trigonometry (Kelland's or Playfair's Euclid).
4. Logarithms.

Second Year.

CLASS BOOKS.

1. Euclid, B. XI., 1-21, 33 ; and XII., 1, 2.
2. Snowball's Plane and Spherical Trigonometry.
3. Whewell's Conic Sections.
4. Hall's Differential and Integral Calculus. Examples in Weale's Treatises.
1. Potter's Mechanics.
2. Draper's Natural Philosophy.

Third Year.

CLASS BOOKS.

1. Evans' Newton's Principia, first three sections.
2. Hydrostatics (Phear).
3. Astronomy (Galbraith & Haughton).

Additional for honors.

Earnshawe's Statics and Dynamics, first four chapters in each.

LOGIC, MENTAL AND MORAL PHILOSOPHY, AND RHETORIC.

Rev. JOHN C. MURRAY, Professor.

Regular Students in Arts are required to attend these Classes during the third Session of their Academic course.

At the Degree examination, candidates will be examined in the following books, as well as in the lectures :—

Whately's Logic, Book II.

Hamilton's Lectures on Metaphysics, XI.-XX. inclusive.

Alexander's Moral Science.

Whately's Rhetoric, Part I.

Spalding's English Literature, Part III.

Candidates for honors must submit to an additional examination in Hamilton's Lectures on Metaphysics, XXVIII.—XLVI. inclusive.

For summer work are proposed:—1. As a subject of study, Aristotle's Nicomachean Ethics, Book X.; 2. As a subject of Essay, "The Moral Consciousness analyzed into its component elements of Cognition and Feeling."

A prize is offered for superiority in each of these, and is open to all regular Students of this Class during the past Session. The Essays and the names of those who intend to undergo examination on the subject of study, must be given in to Professor MURRAY before the 15th of November.

NATURAL SCIENCE.

GEORGE LAWSON, PH.D., LL.D., Professor.

Regular Students in Arts are required to attend during their first Academic Session a preliminary course of Natural History on Tuesdays and Fridays, and the whole of the Natural History Course during their second Session; but occasional Students and those in other Faculties may take either the whole course or any of the subjects separately. Fee for the whole course, $12. For Botany, Zoology or Geology, separately, $4 each.

	MONDAY, 11–12.	TUESDAY, 11–12.	WEDNES., 11–12.	THURS., 11–12.	FRIDAY, 11–12.
During the months of Oct'r, Nov'r, and Dec'r, 1863.	Histology.	Botany.	Botany.	Zoology.	Zoology
During Jan., Feb., March and April, 1864.	Mineralogy.	Geology.	Geology.	Zoology.	Botany.

During the month of October the Botanical Class will meet in the Botanic Garden for open-air Demonstrations as frequently as the weather may permit; during the month of March the Mineralogical Class will meet in the Laboratory for the chemical examination of Minerals; and during February and April, the Geological Class will meet frequently in the Museum.

CLASS BOOKS.

Botany : Balfour's Outlines, or Gray's Text Book.

Zoology : Dallas's Natural History of the Animal Kingdom, or Agassiz & Gould's Comparative Physiology.

Geology : Dana's Manual of Geology, or Page's Text Books.

DESCRIPTIVE AND FIELD BOOKS.

Gray's Manual of Botany of the Northern States ; Nichol's or Dana's Mineralogy ; Reports and other publications of the Geological Survey of Canada ; Davies's Naturalist's Guide ; Carpenter on the Microscope.

GRADUATION IN ARTS AND THEOLOGY.

The Curriculum and Examinations necessary for the Degree of B.A. are the following :—

I. CURRICULUM.

First year.—Junior Latin and Greek, Junior Mathematics and Junior Natural History.

Second year.—Senior Latin and Greek, Senior Mathematics, Natural Philosophy and Senior Natural History.

Third year.—Third Latin and Greek, Third Mathematics, Natural Philosophy and Mental and Moral Philosophy.

II. EXAMINATIONS.

1. Matriculation examination at the beginning of the first Session. If this be successfully passed, the Student ranks as an Under-graduate, and as such, must undergo the subsequent University examinations as part of the course. The fee for matriculation is $4. For subjects see page 12.

2. Primary examination at the close of the first Session. The books and subjects are those given under the different

classes for the first year, with the addition of the following extra subjects :—

The four Gospels and the Acts in English.
Bullion's larger English Grammar, Syntax.
Spalding's English Literature, Part I.
White's Eighteen Christian Centuries. First five Centuries.

3. Previous Examination at the close of the second Session. The books and subjects are those given under the different Classes for the second year, with the addition of the following extra subjects :—

Gospel by Luke in Greek.
Spalding's English Literature, Part II.
White's Eighteen Christian Centuries. The 6th to the 13th inclusive.
Paley's Natural Theology.

4. Final or Degree examination at the close of the third Session. The books and subjects are the same as those given under the different classes, with the addition of the following extra subjects :—

Epistle to the Ephesians in Greek.
White's Eighteen Christian Centuries. The 14th to the 18th inclusive.
Paley's Evidences, Part I.

The examinations will be partly *viva voce* and partly in writing.

Under-graduates who pass the examinations will, at the close of each Session, receive pass or honor certificates in each department, according to their standing.

The Degree of M.A. can be taken only after an interval of two years from the date of graduation as B.A. The candidate must compose a satisfactory thesis on a professional or other subject selected by himself and approved by the Faculty. The fee for B.A. is $10, and for M.A. $20.

Students from other Universities may be admitted *ad eundem statum*, by producing certificates of attendance. Fee, $4.

Graduates from other Universities may be admitted *ad eundem gradum ;* but evidence must, in all cases, be produced that the candidate has gone through a curriculum of Collegiate attendance equivalent to that of Queen's College. Fee for B.A. $10, and for M.A. $20.

4

Graduates will be ranked in three classes. 1. Those who simply pass. 2. Those who pass with honors. 3. Those who pass with highest honors. A Student is not entitled to highest honors unless he has gained honors in each of the departments, of Classics, Mathematics, Natural History, Moral Philosophy, and English Literature.

No honorary Degrees in Arts are conferred.

The Degrees of D.D. and LL.D. are honorary, and are given for literary, scientific and professional distinction.

The Degree of B.D. is conferred each Session on the third year's Student of Divinity who stands highest at the University examination on the subjects of the lectures during the Session, provided he attain an adequate standard of excellence. The Degree of B.A. must have been previously taken.

COLLEGE AND GRAMMAR SCHOOL.

The College Preparatory School and the Kingston County Grammar School are now united and affiliated to the University.

Classical Master	... ...	SAMUEL WOODS, B.A.
Mathematical Master	... ...	THOMAS GORDON.
English Master	... ...	ALFRED LeRICHEUX.
French Master	... ...	MONS. TANNER.
Drawing Master	... ...	MR. LIGHT.

FEES PER TERM.

1. Common English Branches, &c.	... ...	$4 00
2. Junior Classics, Mathematics, &c.	... ...	6 00
3. Senior Classics, Mathematics, &c.	... ...	8 00
4. Drawing	... ...	2 50

Winter Term begins 7th January.
Spring Term begins first Wednesday after Easter.
Summer Term begins second Monday of August.
Autumn Term begins on Monday after 15th October.

This School being now provided with a full and efficient staff of Masters, is qualified to give a thorough Grammar School education and prepare for the University.

Mr. GORDON is prepared to receive a limited number of Boarders.

SCHOLARSHIPS.

CAMPBELL SCHOLARSHIP.

Value, £20. Open, once every three years, to all the pupils of the Kingston Grammar School. Tenable for the first year of the Arts course in Queen's College. First Session tenable 1864-5. Examination in the matriculation subjects of Queen's College.

WATKINS SCHOLARSHIP.

Value, £20. Open to all the pupils of the College Grammar School. Tenable for the first year of the Arts course in Queen's College. Competitive examination on the matriculation subjects of Queen's College.

QUEEN'S SCHOLARSHIPS.

There are three, of the yearly value of £10. Open to all the pupils of the College Grammar School. Tenable for the first year of the Arts course in Queen's College. Competitive examination on the matriculation subjects of Queen's College.

QUEEN'S SCHOLARSHIPS.

There are ten, of the yearly value of £7 10s. Open to all pupils of the Common Schools of Kingston. Tenable for two years at the College Grammar School. Competitive examinations on subjects taught in the Common Schools.

CHAIRMAN'S SCHOLARSHIP.

Value, £7 10s. yearly. Open to all pupils of the Common Schools of Kingston, and tenable for two years at the Grammar School. Competitive examinations on subjects taught in the Common Schools. Founded jointly, for two years, by THOS. KIRKPATRICK, Esq., Chairman of the Board of Trustees of the Grammar School, and WM. FORD, Esq., Chairman of the Board of Common School Trustees.

The following is the deed of the Campbell Scholarship, which is given as a guide to those who may desire to connect any Grammar School in which they are interested with Queen's College :—

KNOW ALL MEN BY THESE PRESENTS, that I, ————— —————, Member of the Legislative Council of the Province of Canada for the Division of —————, am held and firmly bound unto "Queen's College" at Kingston in the penal sum of one hundred pounds of the lawful money of Canada, to be paid to the said Queen's College at Kingston, or their certain Attorney, for which payment well and truly to be made I bind myself firmly by these presents, sealed with my seal and dated the tenth day of February, in the year of our Lord one thousand eight hundred and sixty-two. And whereas I am desirous of creating a Scholarship in the University of Queen's College of the annual value of twenty pounds, to continue to exist during the term of my holding the office or position of Member of the Legislative Council for the Division of —————, and to be called " The ————— Scholarship"—such Scholarship to be subject to and held under the following rules, namely :—

I. The annual value of the Scholarship shall be —————.

II. It shall be held for one year only, which year shall be the first of the curriculum at Queen's College.

III. The Scholarship shall be held in rotation by a pupil from one of the three Grammar Schools in Cataraque Division, and in the following order, namely:—"The Newburgh Grammar School," "The Bath Grammar School," "The Kingston County Grammar School."

IV. The Scholarship shall be open to any pupil who has been in the Grammar School for one year or upwards.

V. Candidates for the Scholarship shall be examined in the Grammar School at one of the regular examinations by the Head Master of the Grammar School and an Examiner appointed by Queen's College. The examination may be written or oral, or both, as the Examiners may deem proper.

VI. The subjects of examination shall be those of the Matriculation examination of Queen's College.

VII. The Scholarship shall not be awarded by the Examiners if, in their opinion, none of the candidates have acquitted themselves satisfactorily.

VIII. In the event of the Examiners reporting to Queen's College that no candidate has entitled himself to the Scholarship, the same shall for that year be at the disposal of the Senate of Queen's College, to be by them given to the most deserving freshman of the year. Other things being equal, a student having the surname of ———— shall be preferred.

Now, the condition of this obligation is such, that if the said ———————— do and shall in each year during the next five (of which this present year of our Lord one thousand eight hundred and sixty-two shall be reckoned one, should he so long continue to be the Member for the Division of ———— in the Legislative Council of this Province), on the first day of the month of September in each year, pay to Queen's College at Kingston, or their Attorney in that behalf, the sum of twenty pounds, to be by the University applied for the purpose and in the manner herein provided, then this obligation shall be void, but otherwise shall remain in full force.

(Signed)

PLAN OF STUDIES PURSUED AT THE KINGSTON COUNTY GRAMMAR SCHOOL.

	CLASSICS.	ARITHMETIC.	ALGEBRA.	EUCLID.	MENSURAT'N.	HISTORY AND GEOGRAPHY.	GRAMMAR.	READING.	
Form I.	Arnold's Accidence and First Book.	Fractions and Proportion.				Outlines of Geography and History.	Elements of English Grammar.	IV. Book and Spelling.	Writing.
Form II.	Arnold's First and Second Book, with Fables.	Practice, Interest and Percentage.	Simple Equations.	Book I.		Geography, History of England.	English Grammar.	IV. Reader and Derivation.	Writing.
Form III.	Edin. Lat. Gram.; Cæsar; Greek Accidence; Latin Composition.	End of Section IX., Sangster's Arithmetic.	Colenso's, to the end of Quadratics.	Books II. & III.	Mensurat'n of Superficies.	Geography; History of England, " Rome.	Grammar and Composition.	V. Reader.	Writing.
Form IV.	Edin. Gk. Gram.; Latin Composit'n; Sallust, Virgil; Greek Compos'n, Xenophon.	Sangster's Arithmetic, to the end.	Colenso's Algebra, Part I.	Books IV. & VI.	Mensurat'n of Solids.	Phys'l and Math'l Geography; Clas'l Geography; History of Rome, Greece and Engl'd.	Analysis of Eng. Classical Authors and Composition.		Writing.

QUEEN'S SCHOLARS AT GRAMMAR SCHOOL.

James E. Burgess,	Thos. Alexander,
John Matthews,	John Orr,
J. A. McDowall,	John Farthing,
C. E. McIntyre,	R. Crawford,
Wm. H. Fuller,	Thos. O. Butler.

CHAIRMAN'S SCHOLAR.

T. W. Hugo.

. The curriculum
must attend
Criticism,

ACT OF THE
CANADA
All Sc...
connection

...

thereon, to
who are
then compear
examination on the
The subjects of exam...
I. In Latin. To
of Horace, and in the
tions on the scanning,
To write a few paragraph...
II. In Greek. To
Books of the Iliad, and in
To write a few sentences
III. Mathematics. The
Trigonometry, and Algebra as far as
IV. Logic, Moral and Natural
V. General Knowledge, as
History.
VI. Composition. A specimen of
English Composition, by writing in a
moral or general subject

THEOLOGICAL FACULTY.

The Very Rev. WILLIAM LEITCH, D.D., Principal and Primarius Professor.

The Session opens on the first Wednesday of November, and closes on the last Thursday of April.

The curriculum extends over three years. The Student must attend Divinity, Hebrew, Church History and Biblical Criticism, each three Sessions.

ACT OF THE SYNOD OF THE PRESBYTERIAN CHURCH OF CANADA IN CONNECTION WITH THE CHURCH OF SCOTLAND.

All Students of Divinity of the Presbyterian Church of Canada in connection with the Church of Scotland, who shall be candidates for license to preach the Gospel, as also all Students of Divinity, Probationers, or Ministers from Churches not in connection with the Presbyterian Church of Canada in connection with the Church of Scotland, desirous of joining this Church, shall, first, place their Certificates of Character and of Literary and Theological Curriculum on the Table of the Presbytery of the bounds within which they reside, who shall examine the same, and decern—and, if sustained, shall transmit the same, with their Deliverance thereon, to the Synod at its next meeting or to the Examining Committee, who are authorised to receive and act on the same. The applicant shall then compear before the Examining Committee and undergo a thorough examination on the several branches of education required by this Church.

The subjects of examination shall be as follows :—

I. IN LATIN. To read, *ad aperturam libri*, in the Odes and Epodes of Horace, and in the Orations of Cicero against Cataline, with examinations on the scanning, parsing, &c.

To write a few paragraphs of Latin, from English dictated.

II. IN GREEK. To read in the Greek New Testament, in the first Six Books of the Iliad, and in the Anabasis of Xenophon.

To write a few sentences of Greek, from English dictated.

III. MATHEMATICS. The first Six Books of Euclid, Elements of Plane Trigonometry, and Algebra as far as Quadratic Equations.

IV. LOGIC, MORAL AND NATURAL PHILOSOPHY.

V. GENERAL KNOWLEDGE, as Geography and the leading facts of History.

VI. COMPOSITION. A specimen of the applicant's ability in respect of English Composition, by writing in a certain time a short Essay on some moral or general subject.

5

VII. In Theology. 1. The Evidences of Christianity. 2. The peculiar Doctrines of the Gospel; the harmony and difference between the Jewish and Christian systems. 3. Difference between the Calvinistic and Arminian systems. 4. The principles of Presbyterian polity and Church Government. 5. A general view of the great outlines of Church History, and especially of the Church of Scotland. 6. Hebrew and Chaldaic,—the principles of the grammar, and of Hebrew Poetry,—and to read portions both of the Hebrew and Chaldee parts of the Old Testament.

The following are the six regular discourses :—

First Year.—Homily and Exegesis.

Second Year.—Lecture and Greek exercise.

Third Year.—Sermon and Hebrew exercise.

The above order, except in special cases, is to be observed.

The following are the subjects of lecture for Session 1863–4 :

Systematic Theology.—Being and Attributes of God; The Trinity ; Inspiration ; Reason and Faith.

Apologetic Theology.—Defences against recent forms of attack.

Pastoral Theology.—Homiletics.

Subjects of examination in Text Books :—

Hill's Lectures on Divinity, Books II. and III.
Butler's Analogy.—Part I.
Paley's Evidences.—Part I.
Greek Testament.—John's Gospel and Galatians.
The standards of the Church on subjects of lecture and the Sacraments.

The course is so arranged that the Students are examined on the whole of Hill's Lectures, Butler's Analogy, Paley's Evidences, during the three years' curriculum.

I. DIVINITY.

The VERY REVEREND PRINCIPAL LEITCH, D.D., PROFESSOR.

COURSE OF LECTURES.

HOURS.	MONDAY.	TUESDAY.	WEDNESDAY.	THURSDAY.	FRIDAY.
11—12, Lecture.	Systematic Theology.	Systematic Theology.	Systematic Theology.	Apologetic Theology.	Pastoral Theology.
3—4, Examinations, Exercises, Discourses.	Butler's Analogy, Greek Testament.	Written Examinations, Greek Testament.	Paley's Evidences, Greek Testament.	Discourses, Greek Testament.	Standards of Church, Exercises in Pulpit Elocution.

At the meeting from three to four, each Student, in turn, opens with a short devotional service of praise, prayer, and reading of the Scriptures. The third year's Students are formed into a Committee for Missionary work on Sabbath. On Friday, the Convener of the Committee reports the arrangements for the following Sabbath; and the Professors intimate at what places they will be present and take part of the duty along with the Students. It is optional for the first and second year's Students to take part in the Missionary work. On Friday, at three o'clock, the class meets in the Convocation Hall for exercises in elocution. Three short discourses of ten minutes each are delivered memoriter, and the Professors criticise the delivery.

II. Oriental Languages, Biblical Criticism and Church History.

The REVEREND J. B. MOWAT, M.A., Professor.

COURSE OF LECTURES.

HOURS.	MONDAY.	TUESDAY.	WEDNESDAY.	THURSDAY.	FRIDAY.
9—10.	Junior Hebrew.	Junior Hebrew.	Junior Hebrew.	Junior Hebrew.	Junior Hebrew.
10—11.	Chaldee.	3rd Hebrew.	3rd Hebrew.	3rd Hebrew.	3rd Hebrew.
2—3.	Syriac.			Arabic.	
4—5.	Church History.	Biblical Criticism	Biblical Criticism	Church History.	Biblical Criticism
5—6.	2nd Hebrew.	2nd Hebrew.	2nd Hebrew.	2nd Hebrew.	2nd Hebrew.

SUBJECTS OF STUDY.

HEBREW.

First Class.

Gen. I. XL. XLI. ; Judges XI. XII ; Obadiah ; Wolf's Grammar ; Arnold's first Hebrew Book ; Bush's Notes on Genesis.

Second Class.

Jonah I.—IV., Eccles. X.—XII. ; Prov. X.—XIII. ; Is. XV.—XXI. ; Grammar ; Translations of English into Hebrew.

Third Class.

Josh. IX. X. ; Ps. I.—XXV. ; Grammar ; Translations of English into Hebrew.

CHALDEE.

Rigg's Manual ; Dan. II. 4–49, III. ; Ezra IV. 8–24.

SYRIAC.

Uhlemann's Grammar. Extracts from the New Testament.

ARABIC.

Stewart's Grammar. Extracts from the Old Testament.

BIBLICAL CRITICISM.

Epistle to Hebrews in Greek ; Stuart on Hebrews ; Angus's Bible Hand-Book, Part II. Lectures.

CHURCH HISTORY.

Kurtz's Text Book, Vol. II. ; 17th, 18th and 19th centuries. Lectures.

FACULTY OF MEDICINE.

FACULTY OF MEDICINE.

VERY REV. WILLIAM LEITCH, D.D.,
Principal and President of the Medical Faculty.

JOHN R. DICKSON, M.D.,
Professor of the Principles and Practice of Surgery, Dean of the Faculty.

HORATIO YATES, M.D.,
Professor of the Principles and Practice of Medicine.

FIFE FOWLER, M.D., L.R.C.S., Edinburgh,
Professor of Materia Medica and Pharmacy.

J. P. LITCHFIELD, M.D.,
Professor of Forensic and State Medicine.

GEORGE LAWSON, Ph. D., LL.D.,
Professor of Chemistry.

M. LAVELL, M.D.,
Professor of Obstetrics and Diseases of Women and Children.

RODERICK KENNEDY, M.D., L.R.C.S., Edinburgh,
Professor of Anatomy.

OCTAVIUS YATES, M.D.,
Professor of the Institutes of Medicine.

MICHAEL SULLIVAN, M.D.,
Demonstrator of Anatomy.

Certificates of attendance on Classes in the Medical Department of Queen's College are recognised by the University of Edinburgh, the Royal College of Surgeons of Edinburgh, and other licensing bodies.

The Degree of M.D. of this University entitles the holder to the Diploma of the Royal College of Surgeons of London, England, on passing the required examination.

Queen's University and College being incorporated by Royal Charter, Graduates in Medicine are entitled to obtain the Provincial License, to practise Physic, Surgery and Midwifery, by simply presenting their Diploma to a District Judge, identifying themselves on oath as the persons named therein, and paying $4, the fee now paid by British Graduates in Medicine to the Provincial Secretary for a License to practise in the Province.

FACULTY OF MEDICINE.

THE SESSION OF THIS FACULTY COMMENCES ANNUALLY ON THE FIRST
WEDNESDAY OF OCTOBER, AND ENDS ON THE LAST THURSDAY OF
MARCH, BEING THE DAY FIXED FOR GRADUATION.
THE NINTH SESSION WILL BE FORMALLY OPENED ON WEDNESDAY,
7TH OCTOBER, AT 3 O'CLOCK, P.M.

DEGREE OF M. D.

A Candidate for the Degree of M.D. must have been en-
gaged in Medical and Surgical study for four years—the
Medical Session of each year, or *Annus Medicus*, being con-
stituted by Matriculation and Attendance on full courses of
Lectures in at least two classes by separate Professors.

One year's instruction under a respectable Medical Practi-
tioner, previous to attendance on Lectures, and duly certified
to the satisfaction of the Medical Faculty prior to the Student
entering upon his studies, will be received as equivalent to a
year's College attendance, and will, in such cases, constitute
the first *Annus Medicus*. A similar exemption from one
year's attendance on Lectures will be accorded to Graduates
in Arts.

The Candidate must have given regular attendance on full
Courses of Instruction in the following departments of Medical
science, for the periods stated :—

1. Principles and Practice of Surgery,	
2. Theory and Practice of Medicine,	
3. Materia Medica and Pharmacy,	
4. Chemistry,	Two full courses
5. Obstetrics and Diseases of Women and Children,	of six months each.
6. Anatomy,	
7. Institutes of Medicine,	
8. Anatomical Demonstrations,	
9. Forensic and State Medicine,	
10. Clinical Medicine,	Two courses each.
11. Clinical Surgery,	
12. Hospital,	Twelve months.

The above course of study may have been pursued either
wholly in Queen's College, or partly in Queen's College, and

6

partly in some other recognized Medical School. In the latter case, at least one full Session must have been spent in Queen's College, during which at least four of the above six months' courses must have been attended.

Certificates of attendance on Lectures are received from incorporated Medical Schools in the British Dominions, and others recognized by the British Universities and Licensing Colleges. Other certificates of attendance on Lectures will be admitted at the discretion of the Faculty.

Every Candidate must deliver before 15th February of the year in which he proposes to graduate, to the Secretary of the Faculty of Medicine, a Declaration under his own hand that he is twenty-one years of age, or will be so before the day of graduation, accompanied by a certificate of good moral character, a statement of his studies, literary and scientific as well as medical, with proper certificates, and a Thesis composed by himself, and in his own handwriting, to be approved by the Medical Faculty.

The Candidate must have passed a Matriculation Examination in the common branches of English Education, and also on one or more of the following works:—Cæsar's Commentaries; London Pharmacopœia; Gregory's Conspectus; Celsus : De Medicina.

The Classical Examination is not required where the Student produces a certificate of having passed a similar or equivalent Matriculation examination at any other College.

Each Candidate shall be examined both in writing and *viva voce*—first, on Materia Medica, Chemistry, Anatomy and Institutes of Medicine:—these subjects constituting the *Primary Examination;* secondly, on Surgery, Theory and Practice of Medicine, Forensic and State Medicine, Obstetrics, Clinical Medicine, and Clinical Surgery, which are the subjects of the *Final Examination.*

Students who profess themselves ready to submit to the *Primary Examination,* that is, to an examination on the first division of these subjects, at the end of their third year, may be admitted to examination at that time. The *Final Examination,* embracing the second division of subjects, shall not take place until the candidate has completed his fourth or last session.

The *Primary* and *Final Examinations* will commence on the 9th of March in each year, or the first lawful day thereafter, and be concluded before the last Thursday of March, which is the day fixed for Graduation.

Additional papers in Classics or in subjects of the Final Examination will be set for candidates for honors.

The Graduation Fee is $20.

COURSE OF INSTRUCTION IN THE FACULTY OF MEDICINE.

JOHN R. DICKSON, M.D., Dean.

I. PRINCIPLES AND PRACTICE OF SURGERY.

JOHN R. DICKSON, M.D., PROFESSOR.

Lectures daily from 4 to 5 P.M.

Class Books:—Miller's Principles of Surgery, Miller's Practice of Surgery.

Fee for the course (six months) $12.

These Lectures will embrace the Principles and Practice of Surgery, and Surgical Anatomy. The course will be illustrated, by Plates and Models, as well as Pathological Specimens. The Use of Instruments and the Application of Surgical Apparatus and Appliances will be taught. The chief operations will be performed on the Cadaver before the Class.

As the Professor of this branch has been appointed Surgeon of the Provincial Penitentiary, he enjoys increased facilities for imparting thorough instruction in Practical Surgery.

II. THEORY AND PRACTICE OF MEDICINE.
HORATIO YATES, M.D., Professor.

Lectures daily from 3 to 4 P.M.

Class Book:—Wood's Practice of Medicine, or Watson's Practice of Medicine.

Fee for the course (six months) $12.

The whole subject of the Theory and Practice of Medicine will be treated in a systematic manner, and special attention will be directed in this course to Diseases of the Heart and Lungs, and to their physical diagnoses, which will be illustrated by numerous cases in the General Hospital, under the immediate instruction of the Professor, and to which cases every Student may have direct access. Thus the Student will be enabled to obtain a thorough and practical knowledge of this important branch of medical practice.

III. MATERIA MEDICA AND PHARMACY.
FIFE FOWLER, M.D., L.R.C.S., Edinburgh, Professor.

Lectures daily from 9 to 10 A.M.

Class Book:—Neligan on Medicines.

Book of Reference:—Pereira's Materia Medica.

The Professor will illustrate his course by colored drawings and specimens of medicinal plants, and samples of the various drugs, chemicals, &c.

Fee for the course (six months) $12.

IV. FORENSIC AND STATE MEDICINE.
J. P. LITCHFIELD, M.D., Professor.

Lectures on Tuesdays and Fridays from 12 to 1.

Books of Reference:—Guy's Forensic Medicine, Taylor's Medical Jurisprudence.

The Professor of this branch being Medical Superintendent of the Rockwood Lunatic Asylum, will have ample opportunities of instructing his class in the important subject of Psychological Medicine.

Fee for the course (six months) $6.

V. CHEMISTRY.

GEORGE LAWSON, Ph.D., LL.D., Professor.

Lectures daily from 10 to 11 A.M., illustrated by extensive series of diagrams, tables, apparatus and preparations. Experiments daily.

Class Book :—Fownes' Manual of Chemistry, or Gregory's Hand-book.

Laboratory Books :—Fresenius' Qualitative and Quantitative Analysis, Croft's Practical Chemistry, Bowman's Medical Chemistry.

Fee for the course of Lectures (six months) $12.

A separate class for PRACTICAL CHEMISTRY is taught, on Mondays, Wednesdays and Thursdays, from 12 to 1 o'clock. The Laboratory is commodious, comfortably heated, well ventilated, and specially fitted up for convenience in teaching simultaneously a large class. Each Student has the use of a separate set of reagents, and performs every experiment for himself. Instruction is given in manipulation, use and fitting up of apparatus, preparation of reagents, &c., after which a Systematic Course of Testing and Separation of Bases and Acids is gone through, with Special Processes applicable to Medical Chemistry and Toxicology.

The course of Practical Chemistry is not compulsory, but the Faculty strongly recommend Students of Medicine to avail themselves of its advantages. Fee for the course of Practical Chemistry $5, with $2 for use of apparatus and reagents.

Students providing their own materials may work continuously in the Laboratory.

VI. OBSTETRICS AND DISEASES OF WOMEN AND CHILDREN.

MICHAEL LAVELL, M.D., Professor.

Lectures daily from 5 to 6 P.M.

Books of Reference :—Churchill's Midwifery, Churchill on Diseases of Women, West on Diseases of Children.

Fee for the course (six months) $12.

Ample opportunities will be afforded to the Students for studying this important branch practically. The Students will be arranged in classes to attend the Obstetric practice of the Hospital.

VII. INSTITUTES OF MEDICINE.

OCTAVIUS YATES, M.D., Professor.

Lectures daily from 11 to 12.

Books of Reference :—Kirke's or Dalton's Physiology, Jones and Sieveking's Pathological Anatomy, Wood's Therapeutics and Pharmacology, Carpenter's Human Physiology.

Fee for the course (six months) $12.

The lectures of this course, which embrace Physiology, General Pathology and Therapeutics, will be illustrated by vivisections, demonstrations with the microscope, also plates, drawings and specimens from the Museum.

Students who have attended two courses of Anatomy in Queen's College prior to Session 1863-4 will not be required to take this Class, and those who have attended one Session in Anatomy prior to 1863-4 will be required to take it only once.

VIII. ANATOMY.

RODERICK KENNEDY, M.D., L.R.C.S., Edinburgh, Professor.

Lectures daily from 2 to 3 o'clock P.M.

Class Book :—Wilson's Anatomy.

Fee for the course (six months) $12.

Daily Lectures will be delivered by the Professor, illustrated by plates, preparations, and demonstrations on the dead body.

IX. ANATOMICAL DEMONSTRATIONS.

MICHAEL SULLIVAN, M.D., Demonstrator.

Daily demonstrations on the recent subject from 8 to 9 o'clock A.M.

Book for use in Dissecting Room :—Ellis's Demonstrations.

Fee for each course of Anatomical Demonstrations and use of the Dissecting Room (six months) $6.

By an Act of the Province, the bodies of convicts dying in the Provincial Penitentiary are given up for Anatomical purposes. This gives to Kingston very great advantages for the study of Practical Anatomy.

X. HOSPITAL.

The Kingston General Hospital may be attended by Students during their whole period of study by one payment of $4 at the commencement of the course.

'The Hospital, which has been lately enlarged, has accommodation for 150 beds. The recently erected Watkins wing contains a very large and commodious Clinical Lecture Room and Operating Theatre, so arranged as to afford an opportunity to all Students of simultaneously witnessing the operations.

The Lectures on Clinical Medicine and Clinical Surgery will in future be delivered twice a week in the new Theatre of the Hospital. Fee entitling to attendance on both courses $6.

Prof. J. R. DICKSON, M.D., Lecturer on Clinical Surgery.

Prof. HORATIO YATES, M.D., Lecturer on Clinical Medicine.

Students and Under-graduates in Medicine pay an annual Entrance Fee of $2. Payment of this fee entitles to the use of the Library, which is open daily, at 2 o'clock P.M., and remains open for half an hour.

The fees for each of the Medical Classes are payable on entering the class at the commencement of the Session. A Student who has attended two courses in any Medical Class except the Anatomical Demonstrations in Queen's College is entitled to free attendance in such class at any subsequent time.

As a general rule, there are weekly examinations in all the classes.

Any additional information may be obtained on application to Dr. DICKSON, the Dean of the Medical Faculty, or to Professor LAWSON.

FACULTY OF THE LAW

extends over the ......

Students are .... Offices in the

... ... We ...... for a Degree
...... the courses of lectures on the subjects
...... two of the ......

Anatomical Demonstrator, M.B. ....

The Degree of Ll.B. by ...... attending for the
Sessions the Lectures ...... the Law Faculty, and
passing the Matriculation ...... at the beginning of
first Session, and the ...... close of each Sec-
The Matriculation exam ...... be postponed till
second Session, provided ...... attend the Latin el-
the Faculty of Arts along with the Law class, during the first
Session.

...... dent is exempted from the Matriculation examinat-
on producing a certificate that he has undergone an exami-
tion for admission as a Student of the Laws on the Books
the Law Society for Upper Canada, or an equivalent exam
tion in any College.

The Degree of Ll.B. shortens by two years the period
which the Law Student must be articled. Without th
the period is five years; but if the Degree is taken ......
his being articled, it is only three years

FACULTY OF THE LAW.

Hon. ALEXANDER CAMPBELL, Q.C., ... Dean.
JAMES A. HENDERSON, Esq., D.C.L., Master in Chancery... Professor.
WILLIAM GEO. DRAPER, M.A., ... Professor.

COURSE OF INSTRUCTION.

The Law Session begins on the first Monday in January, and extends over the three following months.

The hour for Lecture is from 9 to 10 A.M., so as to admit of Students attending the Arts Classes or Law Offices in the city.

The course of Lectures each year will correspond with the subjects hereinafter given for examination for a Degree.

The Student must pass an examination on the subjects lectured upon each year.

DEGREE OF LL.B.

The Degree of LL.B. is obtained by attending for three Sessions the Lectures delivered by the Law Faculty, and by passing the Matriculation examination at the beginning of the first Session, and the examination at the close of each Session. The Matriculation examination may be postponed till the second Session, provided the Student attend the Latin class in the Faculty of Arts along with the Law class, during the first Session.

A Student is exempted from the Matriculation examination on producing a certificate that he has undergone an examination for admission as a Student of the Laws on the Books of the Law Society for Upper Canada, or an equivalent examination in any College.

The Degree of LL.B. shortens by two years the period for which the Law Student must be articled. Without the Degree the period is five years; but if the Degree is taken *previous to his being articled,* it is only three years.

7

When the lectures are attended during the currency of the articles, the period is not shortened unless the Student has been articled previous to the 1st of March, 1860.

FEES.

The fee for the whole course of Lectures during each Session is $10, which also entitles the Student to the use of the University Library.

The Annual Matriculation Fee is $1.

The Annual Examination Fee is $1.

The fee for Graduation is $10.

SUBJECTS OF EXAMINATION.

MATRICULATION.

1. Odes of Horace—Books I. and III.
2. Euclid—Books I., II. and III.
3. Arithmetic to and including Vulgar Fractions.
4. English Prose Composition.
5. English History and Modern Geography.

LECTURES.

FIRST YEAR.

1. Stephen on Pleading.
2. Blackstone's Commentaries by Stephen, Vol. I.
3. Burton's Compendium of Real Property.

SECOND YEAR.

1. Addison on Contracts.
2. Smith's Mercantile Law.
3. Taylor on Evidence.
4. Chitty on Bills.
5. Statutes of Upper Canada.

THIRD YEAR.

1. Williams on Real Property.
2. Story's Equity Jurisprudence.
3. Pleadings and Practice of the Courts of Law and Equity.
4. Archbold's Landlord and Tenant.
5. Jarman on Wills.
6. Sugden on Vendors and Purchasers.

When the lectures are attended during the currency of the ... tudes, the period is not shortened unless the Student has ... een arrived previous to the 1st of March, 1880.

FEES.

The fee for the whole course of Lectures during each Session ... which also entitles the Student to the use of ... Univer- ... y Library.

The Annual Matriculation Fee is $1.

The Annual Examination Fee is $1.

5. English History and ...

1. Stephen on Pleading.
2. Blackstone's Commentaries ... Stephen, vol. 1
3. Burton's Compendium ... (Property).

1. Addison on Contracts.
3. Taylor on Evidence.
4. Chitty on Bills.
5. Statutes of Upper Canada.

THIRD YEAR.

1. Williams on Real Property ...
2. Story's Equity Jurisprudence.
3. Pleadings and Practice of the Courts of Law and Equity
4. Archbold's Landlord and Tenant.
5. Jarman on Wills.
6. Sugden on Vendors and Purchasers.

Graduates are requested to intimate to the Registrar change of r
or any omissions in the List.

Name	Degree	Year of	Present Residence
Agnew, John	B.A.		Queston.
Anderson, W.J			Tolerman.
Aylsworth, A....			Tamworth
Bain, William			Perth, C.W.
" "			Perth, C.W.
Bain, William R -			rough.
Beckett, James			ton, Ja
Bell, Andrew			Douglas, C.W
Bell, George			Clifton, C.W.
Bell, James M			
, John			
, William			Kingston
Benson, John			Kingston
" "			
Bethune, Alex			Melbourne, A
Bird, F.W			
Bird, Nelson J			Hamilton.
Black, Wm. A.			U.S. Service
Blakeley, Robert			San Francis
Bonner, John			Port Hope, C
			Brankville.
Bourchier, H.P.			
Bowers, S.S.			Valparaiso.
Boyd, Edward			
Boyle, Arthur R			Kingston.
Branigan, F.K.			Port Dalhousie
Bray, John L.	M.D.	1862.	U.S.Service.
Brown, M.J.	M.D.	1863.	Strathroy, C?
Buckley, Philip J.	M.B.	1856.	Waterloo, Kin
Caie, Geo, J.	LL.B.	1863.	Kingston.
Cameron, G.I.	B.A.	1861.	Edinburgh.
Campbell, Alex	B.A.	1861.	Kingston.
Campbell, Donald	B.A.	1862.	Mt. Pleasant, C
	B.A.	1860.	Ottawa.

LIST OF GRADUATES.

Graduates are requested to intimate to the Registrar change of residence or any omissions in the List.

Name.	Degree.	Year of Graduation.	Present Residence.
Agnew, John	B.A.	1859.	Kingston.
Anderson, W. J.	M.D.	1861.	Inkerman.
Aylsworth, Arch. K.	M.D.	1863.	Tamworth.
Bain, William	B.A.	1845.	Perth, C.W.
" "	M.A.	1847.	Perth, C.W.
Bain, William R.	B.A.	1863.	Scarborough.
Beckett, James	M.D.	1863.	Kingston, Jamaica.
Bell, Andrew	B.A.	1853.	Douglas, C.W.
Bell, George	B.A.	1847.	Clifton, C.W.
Bell, James M.	M.D.	1857.	
Bell, John	B.A.	1862.	Kingston.
Bell, William	B.A.	1855.	Kingston.
Benson, John R.	B.A.	1853. }	Melbourne, Austr.
" " "	M.D.	1858. }	
Bethune, Alex.	M.D.	1858.	Hamilton.
Bird, F. W.	M.D.	1859.	U. S. Service.
Bird, Nelson J.	M.D.	1860.	San Francisco.
Black, Wm. A.	M.D.	1862.	Port Hope, C.W.
Blakeley, Robert	M.D.	1861.	Frankville.
Bonner, John,	B.A.	1845. }	New York.
" "	M.A.	1847. }	
Bourchier, H. P.	B.A.	1853.	Valparaiso.
Bowers, S. S.	M.D.	1857.	
Boyd, Edward	LL.B.	1863.	Kingston.
Boyle, Arthur R.	M.D.	1859.	Port Dalhousie.
Branigan, P. K.	M.D.	1862.	U. S. Service.
Bray, John L.	M.D.	1863.	Strathroy, C.W.
Brown, M. J.	M.D.	1856.	Waterloo, Kingston.
Buckley, Philip J.	LL.B.	1863.	Kingston.
Caie, Geo. J.	B.A.	1861.	Edinburgh.
Cameron, C. I.	B.A.	1861.	Kingston.
Campbell, Alex.	B.A.	1862.	Mt. Pleasant, C.W.
Campbell, Donald	B.A.	1850.	Ottawa.

Name.	Degree.	Year of Graduation.	Present Residence.
Campbell, George	M.D.	1859.	H. M. Navy.
Campbell, John	B.A.	1847.	Nottawasaga.
" "	M.A.	1850.	
Campbell, J. H.	M.D.	1856.	(Deceased.)
Campbell, Robert,	B.A.	1856.	Galt.
" "	M.A.	1858.	
Chambers, Daniel	M.D.	1855.	London, C.W.
Chamberlane, T. F.	M.D.	1862.	Morrisburg.
Chanonhouse, John	M.D.	1863.	Kingston.
Chanonhouse, Thomas	M.D.	1860.	Shannonville.
Chisholm, H. F.	M.D.	1857.	Port Hope.
Cluness, W. R.	B.A.	1855.	Petaluma, California
" "	M.D.	1859.	
Cogan, Jeremiah R.	M.D.	1861.	Lindsay.
Coleman, W. F.	M.D.	1863.	Lynn, C.W.
Corbett, Geo. H.	M.D.	1856.	Orillia.
Corry, Robert	M.D.	1861.	Lanark.
Craig, Wm.	B.A.	1858.	Kingston.
Cranstoun, J. G.	M.D.	1860.	Renfrew.
Crawford, Joseph	M.D.	1856.	Durham.
Curran, Wm. B.	B.A.	1859.	Montreal.
Currie, Archibald	B.A.	1858.	Cote St. George,
" "	M.A.	1861.	Glengarry.
Davis, R. H.	M.D.	1858.	
Dawson, Alex.	B.A.	1859.	Niagara.
Day, B. W.	M.D.	1862.	Kingston.
Day, H. W.	M.D.	1859.	Trenton.
Deans, Wm. C.	M.D.	1861.	California.
Dickson, John R.	M.D.	1863.	Kingston.
Dingwall, James	B.A.	1861.	Kemptville.
Donald, William,	D.D.	1861.	New Brunswick.
Douglas, James	B.A.	1858.	Quebec.
Douglas, Robert	B.A.	1851.	Weston, C.W.
" "	M.D.	1855.	
Drummond, A. T.	B.A.	1860.	Kingston.
" "	LL.B.	1863.	
Dunbar, Neil	B.A.	1854.	Mirrickville.
Dunbar, Samuel	M.D.	1855.	
Dunlop, Neil	M.D.	1861.	Kingston.
Dupuis, Thos. R.	M.D.	1860.	Odessa.
Edmison, Henry	B.A.	1863.	Peterborough.
Elmer, Wm. W.	M.D.	1858.	Madoc.

Name.	Degree.	Year of Graduation.	Present Residence.
Elwell, W. D.	M.D.	1863.	Kingston.
Evans, Henry	M.D.	1858.	(Deceased.)
Evans, Joseph	B.A.	1855.	Lichfield.
" "	M.A.	1857.	
Farrel, J. T.	M.D.	1861.	Oswego.
Fee, Samuel H.	M.D.	1862.	Kingston.
Ferguson, C. F.	M.D.	1859.	Kemptville.
Ferguson, E. G.	M.D.	1863.	Pittsburg.
Ferguson, George	B.A.	1851.	L'Orignal.
Ferguson, James F.	B.A.	1862.	Kingston.
Ferguson, R. B.	M.D.	1863.	Pembroke, C.W.
Ferguson, Thomas	B.A.	1863.	Pittsburg.
Ferguson, Wm. B.	B.A.	1861.	Kingston.
Foster, R. J.	M.D.	1859.	Picton.
Fowler, Fife	M.D.	1863.	Kingston.
Fraleck, E. B.	B.A.	1863.	Belleville.
Franklin, B. W.	M.D.	1856.	
Fraser, Alex. G.	B.A.	1852.	(Deceased.)
Fraser, John M.	B.A.	1855.	Morpeth.
" " "	M.D.	1861.	
Fraser, Joshua	B.A.	1858.	Montreal.
Gildersleeve, James	LL.B.	1863.	Kingston.
Giles, John G.	M.D.	1860.	Farmersville.
Gordon, James	B.A.	1852.	Markham.
" "	M.A.	1854.	
Gordon, John	B.A.	1861.	Pictou, N.S.
Harkness, Thomas F.	B.A.	1861.	Kingston.
Hacket, Joseph	M.D.	1858.	Maple.
Hamilton, David	M.D.	1862.	Kingston.
Hart, Thomas	B.A.	1860.	Perth.
Heenan, Daniel	B.A.	1849.	(Deceased.)
Henderson, Donald	M.D.	1858.	Wardsville.
Henderson, William	D.D.	1862.	Newcastle, N.B.
Henderson, William	M.D.	1859.	Metcalfe.
Herriman, Wm. C.	M.D.	1855.	Orono.
Hillier, William	M.D.	1855.	Enniskillen, C.W.
Hooper, Ed. J.	B.A.	1858.	Camden, East.
" "	M.A.	1861.	
Hope, James A.	B.A.	1862.	Kingston.
Horsey, Ed. H.	M.D.	1860.	Perth.
Howells, Thos. B.	M.D.	1863.	Kingston.
Hunter, Alex.	B.A.	1861.	Elora.

Name.	Degree.	Year of Graduation.	Present Residence.
Ingersoll, Isaac F.	M.D.	1863.	Fredericksburg.
Irwin, C. A.	M.D.	1863.	Toronto.
Jamieson, Alex.	B.A.	1863.	Williamstown.
Jardine, Robert	B.A.	1863.	Brockville.
Johnson, Absalom H.J.	M.D.	1862.	Sydenham.
Johnson, William	B.A.	1850. }	Lindsay.
" "	M.A.	1852. }	
Joy, Sylvanus	M.D.	1857.	Otterville.
Kay, William	M.A.		Goderich.
Kellock, J. D.	M.D.	1862.	Perth.
Kelly, David	M.D.	1861.	Orillia.
Kelly, Ed. J.	M.D.	1861.	Consecon.
Kennedy, Roderick	M.D.	1863.	Kingston.
Kemp, James A.	M.D.	1861.	Port Colborne.
Kincaid, Robert	M.D.	1863.	Peterborough.
Laidlaw, Alex. R.	M.D.	1857.	
Lambert, Robert	M.D.	1859.	Gosfield.
Lavell, Michael	M.D.	1863.	Kingston.
Lawlor, Michael	M.D.	1857.	Toronto.
Lennox, D. (ad eundem)	B.A.	1861.	Smith's Falls.
Lindsay, John	B.A.	1852. }	(Deceased.)
" "	M.A.	1854. }	
Lindsay, Peter	B.A.	1851.	Arnprior.
Litchfield, John P.	M.D.	1863.	Kingston.
Livingston, John	B.A.	1857.	(Deceased.)
Lochead, John S.	B.A.	1861. }	North Gower.
" "	M.A.	1863. }	
Machar, John, M.A.	B.A.	1857.	Kingston.
Malloch, Archibald	B.A.	1862.	Brockville.
Malloch, E. G.	B.A.	1860.	Perth.
Malloch, Geo. W.	B.A.	1850.	Brantford.
Mattice, Wm. D.	B.A.	1847.	(Deceased.)
May, John	B.A.	1857. }	Kingston.
" "	M.A.	1861. }	
Meadows, R.W. L.R.C.S.E.	.D.	1862.	Surgeon in H. M. S.
Mercer, J. G.	M.	1855.	
Miller, Thomas	M.D.	1852.	Berlin, C.W.
Miller, Thomas	B.A.	1854.	Flamboro', C.W.
Milligan, George	B.A.	1862.	Kingston.
Moore, Andrew	M.D.	1863.	Shannonville.
Morden, John H.	M.D.	1859.	Brockville.
Morrison, Duncan	B.A.	1862.	Ottawa.

Name.	Degree.	Year of Graduation.	Present Residence:
Mostyn, William	M.D.	1858.	Almonte.
Mowat, John B.	B.A.	1845.	Kingston.
" "	M.A.	1847.	
Mudie, John	B.A.	1863.	
Muir, Alexr.	B.A.	1851.	Scarboro'.
Muir, James C.	D.D.	1858.	South Georgetown.
Muir, James	B.A.	1861.	South Georgetown.
Muir, P. D.	B.A.	1856.	Kingston.
McBain, Alex.	B.A.	1860.	Chatham, C.W.
" "	M.A.	1862.	
McCammon, James	M.D.	1863.	Gananoque.
McCaul, James	B.A.	1859.	Kingston.
Macdonald, Alex.	B.A.	1861.	Kingston.
Macdonald, Alex. R.	M.D.	1857.	Consecon.
Macdonald, Colin	B.A.	1855.	Gananoque.
Macdonald, Donald	B.A.	1854.	Scotland.
Macdonald, Duncan	B.A.	1859.	Kingston.
" "	M.A.	1863.	
Macdonald, H. S.	B.A.	1859.	Gananoque.
" "	M.A.	1861.	
Macdonald, Hon. J. A.	LL.D.	1863.	Kingston.
Macdonnell, Daniel J.	B.A.	1858.	Wardsville.
" "	M.A.	1860.	
Macdonell, George	B.A.	1860.	Toronto.
Macdonell, J. A.	M.D.	1862.	Kingston.
McEwen, James	B.A.	1852.	Westminster, C.W.
" "	M.A.	1854.	
McGillivray, Alex.	D.D.	1858.	(Deceased.)
McGillivray, F.	B.A.	1852.	Williamstown.
McGillivray, Neil	B.A.	1848.	Williamstown.
McIntyre, John	B.A.	1847.	(Deceased.)
McIntyre, John	B.A.	1861.	Kingston.
McKay, Wm. Ed.	B.A.	1856.	Orangeville, C.W.
McKellar, Dugald	M.D.	1855.	Embro.
McKenzie, Andrew	M.D.	1862.	Ottawa.
McKenzie, Edward	M.D.	1860.	Pembroke.
McKenzie, J. A.	B.A.	1856.	Goderich.
McKerras, J. H.	B.A.	1850.	Bowmanville.
" "	M.A.	1852.	
McLaren, James	B.A.	1850.	Pickering.
McLaren, John	B.A.	1860.	Williamstown.
McLaren, Peter	B.A.	1854.	Lanark, C.W.

58

Name.	Degree.	Year of Graduation.	Present Residence.
McLean, D. J.	B.A.	1855.	Kitley.
McLean, C. R.	M.D.	1859.	U. S. Service.
McLean, Thomas F.	M.D.	1863.	Goderich.
McLennan, Donald	B.A.	1848.	Guelph.
" "	M.A.	1862.	
McLennan, D. B.	M.A.	1861.	Cornwall, C.W.
McLennan, James	B.A.	1849.	Toronto.
McLennan, James	B.A.	1862.	Lancaster.
McLennan, John	B.A.	1855.	Lindsay.
McLennan, K.	B.A.	1849.	Whitby.
McLeod, James A. F.	B.A.	1854.	Bowmanville.
McMillan, Duncan	B.A.	1857.	London, C.W.
McMillan, John	B.A.	1862.	Pictou, N.S.
McMorine, J. K.	B.A.	1859.	Ramsay.
" "	M.A.	1863.	
McNab, F. F.	B.A.	1859.	Picton.
Macpherson, A. J.	M.D.	1862.	Lancaster.
Macpherson, Henry	B.A.	1851.	Owen Sound.
Macpherson, James P.	B.A.	1857.	Cobourg.
McQuarrie, Alex. R.	B.A.	1862.	Pictou, N.S.
Nelles, Samuel S.	D.D.	1861.	Cobourg.
Nichol, James	M.D.	1863.	Perth, C.W.
Noel, John V.	B.A.	1863.	Kingston.
Oliver, Alfred S.	M.D.	1863.	Kingston.
O'Reilly, Anthony	M.D.	1861.	Ottawa.
Parker, Robert	M.D.	1861.	Stirling.
Perrault, Julien	M.D.	1857.	Quebec.
Pope, Stephen D.	B.A.	1861.	Stirling.
Price, Cornelius V.	LL.B.	1863.	Kingston.
Ramsay, Robert	M.D.	1861.	Aurora.
Reily, Adrian	M.D.	1862.	Welland.
Roche, Wm. P.	M.D.	1860.	Inkerman.
Rogers, R. V.	B.A.	1861.	Kingston.
Rollo, James	B.A.	1852.	Toronto.
Rose, George R.	B.A.	1854.	Smith's Falls.
" "	M.D.	1860.	
Rose, George S.	B.A.	1856.	
Ross, Donald	B.A.	1860.	Martintown
" "	M.A.	1862.	
" "	B.D.	1863.	
Ross, John Reid	B.A.	1862.	Thorah.
Ross, Thomas K.	M.D.	1863.	Bath, C.W.

Name.	Degree.	Year of Graduation.	Present Residence.
Ross, Walter	B.A.	1859.	Beckwith.
" "	M.A.	1862.	
Ross, William A.	B.A.	1855.	Ottawa.
Ruttan, Joseph B.	M.D.	1863.	
Scott, W. S.	M.D.	1855.	
Shier, James	B.A.	1863.	Bath, C.W.
Shirley, Joseph W.	M.D.	1863.	Louisville, Kent'ky.
Sievewright, James	B.A.	1855.	Ormstown.
Skinner, Henry	M.D.	1862.	Kingston.
Smith, George	M.D.	1858.	Bristol.
Smith, James C.	B.A.	1861.	Kingston.
" "	M.A.	1863.	
Smith, John R.	M.D.	1863.	U.S. Service.
Sommerville, Jas. A.	B.A.	1859.	Strathroy.
Spafford, H. W.	M.D.	1855.	Newburg, Camden.
Sparham, George S.	M.D.	1859.	Waterloo.
Spencer, Henry	M.D.	1862.	
Spooner, George D.	M.D.	1860.	Percy.
Sproat, Alex.	B.A.	1853.	Southampton.
Squire, William W.	B.A.	1854.	Montreal.
Sullivan, Michael	M.D.	1858.	Kingston.
Sullivan, Thomas	M.D.	1863.	Kingston.
Sullivan, William	B.A.	1862.	Kingston.
Sutherland, Robert	B.A.	1852.	Walkerton, C.W.
Sweetland, John	M.D.	1858.	Pakenham.
Switzer, W. J.	M.D.	1862.	Camden.
Tarbell, H. S. (ad eun.)	B.A.	1862.	Belleville.
Taylor, William F.	M.D.	1861.	Franklin, C.E.
Thibodo, A. J., M.D.,	B.A.	1851.	Walla-walla.
" "	M.A.	1854.	
Thibodo, Oliver	M.D.	1857.	Walla-walla.
Thibodo, Robert	M.D.	1862.	Walla-walla.
" "	B.A.	1862.	
Thibodo, William B.	B.A.	1862.	Kingston.
Thirkell, William G.	M.D.	1861.	Drummondville.
Thomson, George	B.A.	1863.	Kingston.
Thomson, John	B.A.	1855.	Napanee.
Tracey, Robert	M.D.	1862.	Kingston.
Trousdale, James D.	M.D.	1860.	Melrose, C.W.
Walbridge, A. F.	B.A.	1854.	Newcastle, C.W.
Wallace, Alexander	B.A.	1847.	Huntingdon.
Watson, Andrew	B.A.	1861.	Williams.

Name.	Degree.	Year of Graduation.	Present Residence.
Watson, Charles V.	M.D.	1863.	Bloomfield, C.W.
Watson, David	B.A.	1850.	
" "	M.A.	1852.	Thorah, C.W.
Watson, Donald	B.A.	1851.	(Deceased.)
Watson, Peter	B.A.	1852.	Williamstown.
Weir, William	M.D.	1861.	Toledo.
Willis, Michael, D.D.,	LL.D.	1863.	Toronto.
Wilson, John A.	M.D.	1863.	Kingston.
Yates, Horatio	M.D.	1863.	Kingston.
Yates, Octavius	M.D.	1856.	Kingston.
Yeomans, George A.	B.A.	1863.	Odessa.
Yeomans, Horace P.	B.A.	1860.	
" "	M.D.	1863.	Odessa.
Young, Daniel	M.D.	1862.	Bath.

SUMMARY.

Graduates, whole number	..	..	..	260
" in Arts	..	..	..	134
" in Medicine	..	..	..	122
" in Theology	..	..	..	6
" in Law	..	..	..	7
Degrees, whole number	..	..	..	299

LIST OF STUDENTS IN SESSION 1862-3.

FACULTY OF ARTS.

No. in Register.	Name.	Year in Curriculum.	Present Residence.
511	Buckley, Charles	1,	Kingston.
512	Dickson, John	1,	Kingston.
509	Fraser, James	1,	Quebec.
465	Grey, James M.	1,	Kingston.
507	Malloch, George	1,	Ottawa.
513	Meagher, Augustus	1,	Kingston.
503	Muckleston, John S.	1,	Kingston.
510	McAlister, John	1,	Kingston.
506	McBean, Alexander G.	1,	Lancaster.
508	McGregor, Alexander	1,	Glengarry.
505	McKay, Donald	1,	Wolfe Island.
504	McMorine, Samuel	1,	Almonte.
502	O'Loughlin, Robert	1,	Kingston.
501	Thompson, John R.	1,	Charleton, P. E. I.
313	Agnew, Andrew	2,	Kingston.
462	Bell, Josiah I.	2,	Carleton Place.
463	Bethune, William	2,	Cornwall.
464	Fraser, Donald	2,	Glengarry.
460	Mullen, Elias	2,	Chatham.
536	McAulay, Donald	2,	London, C.W.
467	McGeachy, William	2,	Bowmanville.
468	McGillivray, Daniel	2,	Pictou, N.S.
471	McLennan, William	2,	Lancaster.
461	Rennaud, Allen C.	2,	Kingston.
440	Tanner, Charles A.	2,	Montreal.
325	Wylie, James	2,	Almonte, C.W.
23	Bain, William R.	3,	Scarborough.
315	Cameron, John	3,	London, C.W.
316	Edmison, Henry	3,	Peterborough.
317	Ferguson, Thomas B.	3,	Pittsburgh.
318	Fraleck, Baldwin	3,	Belleville.
319	Jamieson, Alexander	3,	Williamstown.
320	Jardine, Robert	3,	Brockville.
321	McAulay, Evan	3,	London, C.W.

No: in Register.		Year in Curriculum.	Present Residence.
323	Noel, John V.	3,	Kingston.
354	Thomson, George	3,	Kingston.
326	Yeomans, George A.	3,	Odessa.

FACULTY OF THEOLOGY.

345	Milligan, George	1,	Kingston.
341	McDonald, Alexander	1,	
343	McMillan, John	1,	Pictou, N.S.
344	McQuarrie, Alexander	1,	Pictou, N.S.
350	Ross, John R.	1,	Bowmore.
339	Cameron, Charles I.	2,	Priceville, C.W.
333	Goodwill, John	2,	Antigonish, N.S.
334	Gordon, John	2,	Pictou, N.S.
335	Hamilton, William	2,	Beauharnois, C.E.
13	Hart, Thomas	2,	Perth, C.W.
338	Hunter, Alexander	2,	Leith, C.W.
472	Lamont, Hugh	2,	Bowmore, C.W.
17	McCaul, James	2,	Kingston.
351	Smith, James C.	2,	Kingston.
307	Barr, John	3,	St. Catherines.
306	Dawson, Alexander	3,	Niagara, C.W.
31	Fraser, Joshua	3,	Montreal.
312	McDonald, Duncan	3,	Kingston.
308	McMorine, John B.	3,	Almonte, C.W.
310	Robertson, John D.	3,	Kingston.
300	Ross, Donald	3,	Charlottenburg.

FACULTY OF MEDICINE.

530	Allen, George Courtney	1,	H. M. Service.
515	Armstrong, Alfred	1,	Kingston.
535	Beattie, William	,	Kingston.
518	Campbell, Joseph	,	Perth, C.W.
512	Dickson, John		Kingston.
527	Ellerbeck, Charles H.	1,	Kingston.
531	Fortune, Lewis	1,	Huntingdon, C. E.
318	Fraleck, E. Baldwin		Belleville.
529	Hickey, Daniel C.	1,	Kingston.
340	Malloch, A. E., B.A.	1,	Brockville.
519	Massie, John	1,	Seymour.
528	Monro, John Campbell	1,	South Finch, C.W.
533	McKee, Thomas	1,	Kingston.
526	Nesbit, Edward	1,	Almonte, C.W.
532	O'Connor, Roderick	1,	Kingston.

No. in Register.	Name.	Year in Curriculum.	Present Residence.
524	Price, R. B.	1,	Bath.
537a	Saunders, Lawrence		Portsmouth, C.W.
537	Shurtleff, Robert Fulton		Ernestown, C.W.
473	Bell, Alexander	2,	Perth, C.W.
327	Bell, John, B.A.	2,	Kingston.
523	Corbett, Henry	2,	Kingston.
474	Darragh, Robert J.	2,	Elginburg, C. W.
499	Deans, George	2,	Trenton.
520	Ferguson, John A.	2,	Toronto.
486	Horsey, Alfred J.	2,	Kingston.
517	Kertland, Edwin H.	2,	Kingston.
497	Morden, James B.	2,	Prince Edward.
494	Muir, Thomas	2,	Kingston.
380	McIntyre, John F.	2,	Portsmouth.
521	McLaren, Alexander	2,	Williamstown.
489	Neish, James		Kingston.
478	Nugeut, Robert J. S.	2,	Bath, C.W.
525	Reeve, Richard A., B.A.	2,	Toronto.
522	Robb, James	2,	Toledo, C.W.
490	Rourke, Francis	2,	Kingston.
488	Wafer, Francis M.	2,	Pittsburg.
477	Weeks, William .J	2,	Brockville.
420	Agnew, John, B.A.	3,	Kingston.
438	Anderson, Thomas	3,	Heckston, C.W.
255	Bigham, Hugh	3,	FenelonFalls,C.W.
534	Bredin, Hawtry	3,	Milford.
267	Brownley, Charles	3,	Kingston Mills.
437	Davidson, Myers	3,	Yarker, Camden.
439	Fox, Edward C.	3,	Wolfe Island.
370	Gleeson, J. H.	3,	Kingston.
479	Hoare, Walter W.	3,	Adelaide, C.W.
383	Maiden, William P.	3,	Port Hope, C.W.
385	Millener, W. S.	3,	Kingston.
481	McIntyre, Duncan	3,	Alvinston.
392	Searls, Abraham W.	3,	Wellington, C.W.
393	Selleck, John	3,	Wellington, C.W.
495	Taylor, James	3,	Bowmanville.
402	Thornton, William M.	3,	Trenton.
403	Tracey, T. B.	3,	Montreal.
404	Wartman, P. G.	3,	Collinsby.
358	Aylsworth, Archibald K.	4,	Tamworth.
359	Beckett, James	4,	Kingston, Ja.

No. in Register.	Name.	Year in Curriculum.	Present Residence.
361	Bigham, John	4,	Orono.
285	Bray, John L.	4,	Strathroy, C.W.
406	Chanonhouse, John	4,	Kingston.
288	Coleman, William F.	4,	Lynn, C.W.
482	Comer, Alex. T. C.	4,	Kingston.
365	Elwell, W. D.	4,	Kingston.
367	Ferguson, Edward G.	4,	Pittsburg.
433	Ferguson, R. B.	4,	Pembroke, C.W.
371	Grasse, Sidney D.	4,	Kingston.
411	Howells, Thomas B.	4,	Kingston.
373	Ingersoll, Isaac F.	4,	Fredericksburg.
374	Irwin, Chamberlen Arthur	4,	Toronto.
428	Kincaid, Robert	4,	Peterborough.
386	Moore, Andrew	4,	Shannonville.
378	McCammon, James	4,	Gananoque.
381	Maclean, Thomas F.	4,	Goderich, C.W.
387	Newton, John	4,	Portsmouth.
484	Ross, Thomas Keith	4,	Bath, C.W.
391	Ruttan, Joseph B.	4,	Kingston.
516	Shirley, Joseph W.	4,	Louisville, Ky.
421	Smith, John R.	4,	Kingston.
398	Sullivan, Thomas	4,	Kingston.
424	Tossell, John	4,	Ottawa.
475	Watson, Charles V., M.D.	4,	Bloomfield, C.W.
405	Wilson, John A.	4,	Kingston.
416	Yeomans, Horace P., B.A.	4,	Waterloo.

FACULTY OF LAW.

No. in Register.	Name.	Year in Curriculum.	Present Residence.
500	Boyd, Edward	3,	Kingston.
442	Buckley, Philip J.	3,	Kingston.
445	Drummond, A. T., B.A.	3,	Kingston.
447	Gildersleeve, James	3,	Kingston.
451	Price, Cornelius V.	3,	Kingston.

SUMMARY.

Matriculated Students in Arts	..	37
" " Theology	..	21
" " Medicine	..	83
" " Law	..	5
		146
Deduct Students in more than one Faculty	..	2
Total number of Matriculated Students	..	144

List of Fellows and Graduates, Session 1862-3.

FELLOWS.

Name.		Faculty elected from.
Drummond, Andrew T., B.A., LL.B.	..	Law.
Machar, John, M.A., Barrister	..	Arts.
Ross, Donald, M.A., B.D.	..	Theology.

GRADUATES.

FACULTY OF THEOLOGY.

B.D.

Ross, Donald, M.A. and Fellow of Queen's University.

FACULTY OF LAW.

LL.D.

Macdonald, Hon. John Alexander, M.P.P.

Willis, Rev. Michael, D.D., Principal of Knox College, Toronto.

LL.B.

Boyd, Edward.   Honors.

Buckley, Patrick Joseph.   Honors.

Drummond, Andrew Thomas, B.A. and Fellow of Queen's University.   Honors.

Gildersleeve, James Philip.   Honors.

Price, Cornelius Valleau.   Honors.

FACULTY OF MEDICINE.

M.D.

The subject of Thesis is given in connection with each name.

Aylsworth, Archibald K.   On Vis Medicatrix Naturæ.

Beckett, James.   On Acetate of Lead.

Bray, John L.

Chanonhouse, John.   On Gonorrhea.

Coleman, William F.

9

Dickson, John R., M.D.
Elwell, W. D.   On Ague.
Ferguson, Edward G.   On Sleep.
Ferguson, Robert B.   On Orchitis.
Fowler, Fife, M.D.
Howells, Thomas B.   On Morbid Sensibility of Stomach and
    Bowels.
Ingersoll, Isaac F.   On Stricture of the Urethra as a consequent
    of Gonorrhea.
Irwin, Chamberlen A.   On Mumps.
Kennedy, Roderick, M.D.
Kincaid, Robert.   On Phthisis.
Lavell, Michael, M.D.
Litchfield, John P., M.D.
Moore, Andrew.   On Signs of Pregnancy.
McCammon, James.   On Copper, its Sources, Properties and
    Applications.
McLean, Thomas F.   On Vegetable Alkaloids.
Oliver, Alfred S.   On Chloroform.
Ross, Thomas K.   On Dysentery.
Ruttan, Joseph B.   On Puerperal Fever.
Shirley, Joseph W.   On Diphtheria.
Smith, John R.   On Digestion.
Sullivan, Thomas.   On Enteric Fever.
Watson, Charles V., M.D.   On Intermittent Fever.
Wilson, John A.   On Disease of the Ovaria.
Yates, Horatio, M.D.
Yeomans, Horace P.   On Spectrum Analysis.

The following candidate passed the necessary examination
for the degree of M.D., which will be conferred on him as
soon as he reaches the required age of twenty-one years :—

Comer, Alexander T. C.

The following Students passed the Primary Examination in
Medicine :

Agnew, John, B.A.	Maiden, William
Anderson, Thomas	Millener, W. S.
Bigham, Hugh	McIntyre, Duncan
Davidson, Myers	Searls, A. W.
Dunn, Thomas Andrew	Taylor, James
Grasse, Sydney	Thornton, W. M.
Hoare, Thomas	Tracey, T. B.

Wartman, P. G.

FACULTY OF ARTS.

M.A.

Lochead, John S., B.A. Thesis: Tudor Period of English History.

McDonald, Duncan, B.A. Thesis: Slavery, as it exists in the United States.

McMorine, John K., B.A. Thesis: War, its causes and consequences.

Smith, James C., B.A. Thesis: American Literature.

B.A.

Bain, William Rutherford.

Edmison, Henry.

Ferguson, Thomas Brooks.

Fraleck, Edison Baldwin. Honors in Natural History.

Jamieson, Alexander. Honors in Natural History.

Jardine, Robert. Honors in Classics, Mathematics, Natural Philosophy, Natural History, Metaphysics and Ethics.

Mudie, John.

Noel, John Vavasseur. Honors in English Literature.

Shier, James.

Thomson, George.

Yeomans, George A.

The following Students passed the University Examinations required for the Degree of B.A. :—

SECOND YEAR.

Agnew, Andrew.

Bell, Josiah J. Honors in Natural History.

Bethune, William. Honors in Classics.

Fraser, Donald. Honors in Natural History and Natural Philosophy.

McAulay, Donald.

McGeachy, William. Honors in Classics, Mathematics, Natural History and Natural Philosophy.

McGillivray, William.

McLennan, William. Honors in Mathematics and Natural Philosophy.

Mullen, Elias.

Rennaud, Allen.

Tanner, Charles.

Wylie, James.

68

Buckley, Charles.
Dickson, John.
Fraser, James.   Honors in Classics.
Gray, James.
Malloch, George.
Muckleston, John.
McAlister, John.
McBean, Alexander.   Honors in Classics.
McGregor, Alexander.
McKay, Donald G.   Honors in Mathematics.
McMorine, Samuel.   Honors in Mathematics.
O'Loughlin, Robert.
Thomson, John R.

Graduates in Theology during the Session		..	11
"	Law	"	"	..	7
"	Medicine	"	"	.	30
"	Arts		"	..	15

53

PRIZE LIST.

FACULTY OF ARTS.
JUNIOR LATIN CLASS.

1 James Fraser,   Quebec, C.E.
2 Alexander G. McBean,   Cornwall, C.W.
3 Robert S. O'Loughlin,   Kingston, C.W.
4 John S. Muckleston,   Kingston, C.W.

ORDER OF MERIT.

John R. Thompson,   Prince Edward Island.
Samuel McMorine,   Ramsay, C.W.

JUNIOR GREEK CLASS.

1 Alexander G. McBean,   Cornwall, C.W.
2 James Fraser,   Quebec, C.E.
3 Samuel McMorine,   Ramsay, C.W.
4. Robert S. O'Loughlin,   Kingston, C.W.

ORDER OF MERIT.

John R. Thompson,   Prince Edward Island.
John S. Muckleston,   Kingston, C.W.

SENIOR LATIN CLASS, JUNIOR DIVISION.

1 William McGeachy,   Bowmanville, C.W.
2 William Bethune,   Cornwall, C.W.
3 Donald Fraser,   Glengarry, C.W.

ORDER OF MERIT.

William McLennan,   Glengarry, C.W.
Daniel McGillivray,   Nova Scotia.

SENIOR GREEK CLASS, JUNIOR DIVISION.

1 William McGeachy,   Bowmanville, C.W.
2 William Bethune,   Cornwall, C.W.
3 Donald Fraser,   Glengarry, C.W.

ORDER OF MERIT.

William McLennan,   Glengarry, C.W.
Daniel McGillivray,   Nova Scotia.

SENIOR LATIN CLASS.

1 Robert Jardine,   Brockville, C.W.
2 Henry Edmison,   Peterboro', C.W.
3 Alexander Jamieson,   Glengarry, C.W.

ORDER OF MERIT.

George Thompson,   Scotland.
George A. Yeomans,   Odessa, C.W.

SENIOR GREEK CLASS.

1 Robert Jardine,   Brockville, C.W.
2 Henry Edmison,   Peterboro', C.W.
3 E. Baldwin Fraleck,   Belleville, C.W.

ORDER OF MERIT.

John Mudie,   Portsmouth, C.W.
Alexander Jamieson,   Glengarry, C.W.

JUNIOR MATHEMATICS.

1 Donald Gordon McKay,   Caithness, Scotland.
2 Samuel McMorine,   Ramsay, C.W.
3 John R. Thompson,   Prince Edward Island.
  Alexander G. McBean,   Glengarry, C.W.
  James Fraser,   Quebec, C.E.
  Alexander McGregor,   Glengarry, C.W.

MATHEMATICS AND NATURAL PHILOSOPHY.

1 { William McGeachy, } Equal. Bowmanville, C.W.
  { Donald Fraser, }   Glengarry, C.W.
2 William McLennan,   Glengarry, C.W.

An Extensive Series of Exercises in various Branches of Mathematics solved during the Summer Recess.—William McGeachy.

Voluntary Essay on "Electricity," written during the Summer Recess.—Josiah Jones Bell, Beckwith, C.W.

SENIOR NATURAL PHILOSOPHY.

Robert Jardine,   Brockville, C.W.

Best Essays on "Optics."—George Thomson, Fifeshire, Scotland; William R. Bain, Scarboro', C.W.

NATURAL HISTORY.

1 William McGeachy,   Bowmanville, C.W.
2 Josiah Jones Bell,   Carleton Place, C.W.

3 Donald Fraser,   Glengarry, C.W.

4 { William McLennan, } Equal.   Glengarry, C.W.
  { Andrew Agnew,   }   Kingston, C.W.

MORAL PHILOSOPHY.

I. For general eminence, awarded by the votes of the Class.

1 George Thomson, B.A.,   Kingston, C.W.
2 William R. Bain, B.A.,   Scarborough, C.W.

II. For eminence in the Written Examinations.

Robert Jardine, B.A.

III. Voluntary Students' Prize.

Donald Ross, M.A., B.D. and Fellow of Queen's University.

FACULTY OF THEOLOGY.

SYSTEMATIC THEOLOGY.

Donald Ross, M.A., B.D. and Fellow of Queen's University, for Missionary duty.

HEBREW.

FIRST CLASS.

John McMillan, B.A.,   Nova Scotia.

SECOND CLASS.

John Gordon, B.A.,   Nova Scotia.

THIRD CLASS.

John K. McMorine, M.A.,   Almonte, C.W.

SCHOLARSHIPS.

The following Scholarships were awarded after competitive examinations on all the subjects of the year of the curriculum. They are tenable during Session 1863-4 :—

THEOLOGICAL FACULTY.

SECOND YEAR.

Charles I. Cameron,   St. Andrew's (Hamilton) Scholarship.

FIRST YEAR.

George Milligan,   St. Andrew's (Montreal) Scholarship.

FACULTY OF ARTS.

THIRD YEAR.

Robert Jardine,	Allan Scholarship.
Henry Edmison,	Montreal Scholarship.
A. Jamieson,	St. Andrew's University Scholarship.

SECOND YEAR.

William McGeachy,	Kingston open Scholarship.
Donald Fraser,	Aberdeen University Scholarship.
William McLennan,	Montreal Scholarship.
Josiah J. Bell,	Foundation open Scholarship.

FIRST YEAR.

A. McBean,	Toronto open Scholarship.
J. Fraser,	Glasgow University Scholarship.
R. O'Loughlin,	Foundation open Scholarship.
A. R. Thompson,	Montreal Scholarship.

In the University examinations, by which the standing of each Student was determined and the Scholarships awarded, the following scheme of marks was adopted.

FACULTY OF ARTS.

FIRST YEAR.	SECOND YEAR.	THIRD YEAR.
Classics 300	Classics 100	Classics 150
Mathematics 150	Mathematics and Natu-	Natural Philosophy ...150
English Literature ... 50	ral Philosophy ...200	English Literature ... 50
	English Literature ... 50	Moral Philosophy ...200
	Natural History ...150	
500	500	550

FACULTY OF THEOLOGY.

Systematic Theology	100
Apologetic Theology	100
Church History	60
Biblical Criticism	90
Hebrew	150
	500

ANNUAL REPORT,

Statements and Treasurer's Accounts,

OF

Queen's University and College,

KINGSTON.

Printed by Order of the Board of Trustees.

ANNUAL REPORT

OF THE

Board of Trustees of Queen's College.

The Trustees of Queen's College beg to submit to the Synod of the Presbyterian Church of Canada in connexion with the Church of Scotland, the following annual report upon the progress and present position of the College, together with detailed financial statements.

The following statement shows the number of Students in the several Faculties at the close of the College Session:—

Arts	37
Theology	21
Medicine	81
Law	5
Total	144

The number of Students in the Arts Faculty studying with a view to the ministry is 18.

During last Session a Code of Statutes, Rules, and Ordinances, for the government of the University, was drawn up and adopted by the Trustees. It was in the power of the Trustees, in accordance with the Royal Charter, to frame such code at the foundation of the College, but it was deemed desirable to wait till experience suggested the most suitable regulations. The University having now expanded so as to embrace the Faculties of Arts, Theology, Law, and Medicine, it was felt that the framing of statutes could no longer be delayed. The Charter gives power to amend the present code or frame new statutes, as experience and the future progress of the College may demand.

Notwithstanding many kind donations and a few purchases from matriculation fees, which are applied to this purpose, the College Library continues very imperfect.

The practical training of Students for the duties of the ministerial office is still carried on with satisfactory results under the care of the Principal. The senior students are employed every Sabbath in addressing audiences at various Stations and Institutions or in teaching Sabbath schools, the Principal and Professors accompanying them in their work. It is found that the pulpit exercises of the Hall do not serve the purpose of such addresses as the above, delivered to actual audiences. The exercises in pulpit elocution, referred to in last report, are still carried on with satisfactory results. An hour is devoted each week to the hearing of short discourses delivered *memoriter* in the Convocation Hall before the Theological Professors, who give their criticism on the delivery. This exercise is found to be of great advantage in giving self-possession and ease of delivery. Defects that may have been unconsciously acquired are pointed out, so that the students are guarded against habits which might seriously mar the efficiency of their pulpit ministrations. Such exercises are of special importance in this country, where an effective pulpit address is essential to the success of a minister.

The Bursary Scheme has not met with that cordial support which was anticipated and which it so deservedly merits. The funds at the disposal of the Trustees have proved quite inadequate to meet the wants of young men studying for the ministry. This is the more to be regretted, as the demand for laborers is rapidly increasing. Constant applications are made for catechists to aid in raising congregations in promising localities which cannot be met for the want of students. This difficulty must be greatly increased if the Bursary Fund fall off. The Lord, in His providence, is loudly calling us to occupy the land and make the waste places rejoice in the Gospel sound; and the most effectual way to respond to this call is to aid a scheme which has for its great end the raising up of men fitted for the work.

The new wing of the Hospital has been completed, and affords accommodation for a large operating theatre and chapel. This wing has been erected by the munificence of a single individual, John Watkins, Esquire, at a cost of upwards of £1,250.

The Observatory is not yet fully equipped; but the Royal Astronomical Society of London has granted the use of an instrument till a permanent transit circle be completed. The Astronomer Royal, Mr. Airy, has kindly undertaken to superintend the execution of a large transit circle, as soon as sufficient funds are secured. The lectures in connection with the Observatory have been attended by very large audiences.

The College has sustained a great loss by the death of the Rev. Dr. Machar, who was a trustee from the foundation of the College, and for several years acted as Principal, and Professor of Hebrew. His practical wisdom, scholarly attainments, and devoted attachment to the Church of Scotland, were of invaluable benefit to the College during its whole history.

Professor John C. Murray was appointed to the chair of Moral and Mental Philosophy at the beginning of last session. He was strongly recommended by the Convener of the colonial committee as the candidate best fitted for the office. Many of the leading men of Scotland also bore the strongest testimony to his qualifications. The spirit of inquiry which he has excited during the past session, and the voluntary attendance of students not belonging to the class, afford evidence that the confidence of the Trustees in his qualifications has not been misplaced.

The University question has advanced a step by the report of the University Commissioners. That report proposes a scheme of University reform which essentially consists of two distinct parts—the one being purely academic, the other financial. The Commissioners applied to the Senate of the University of Toronto and the heads of the various Colleges for suggestions as to the best organization for the advancement of the higher education in Canada, apart altogether from the financial question—the idea being, that if all the bodies agreed as to the academic organization, an important step would be taken in settling the long-vexed financial question. No financial queries were put to the various academic bodies, as this was a matter with which Parliament could best deal. Besides, the financial views of the various bodies were already well known. There was a substantial agreement in the suggestions made by the Senate of the University of Toronto and the various Colleges, and the academic scheme proposed by the Commissioners is based on these suggestions. Its essential character is to have one University Board, in which all the Colleges are equally represented, a common curriculum, and a common examination, so that all students receiving degrees may be subjected to the same test. According to this arrangement, Queen's College would confer degrees in virtue of its Royal charter, but only on students who have passed the examination of the common University Board—the examination taking place at Kingston. The following are the replies of the Senate of Toronto to the queries of the Commissioners in reference to an academic reform:

REPLIES OF SENATE OF UNIVERSITY OF TORONTO TO QUERIES ON AFFILIATION, &c., &c.

QUERY I.—Do you approve of the affiliation of the Colleges of Upper Canada to one University Board, and if so, state the advantages?

I. The Senate are of opinion that it is desirable to have one University Board for Upper Canada, which may be designated "The University of Upper Canada," to which certain Colleges, such as are hereinafter stated, should be affiliated.

Amongst the advantages of this arrangement may be mentioned—the adoption of an uniform and equal course of instruction by such Colleges; the fixing of the value of degrees, the promotion of emulation amongst the affiliated Colleges, and the testing of the merits of different modes of instruction.

QUERY II.—Do you consider the present system of affiliation to the University of Toronto unsatisfactory, and if so, state the reasons?

II. The present system of affiliation under the statute is unsatisfactory, as it is practically inoperative. No sufficient inducements are held out for those Colleges which possess University powers to give up or restrict them. The absence of limitation relative to the number and composition of the Senate is also objectionable.

QUERY III.—What system of affiliation do you consider the most satisfactory, with special reference to the following points:—

(1) The mode of securing an equal standard of education.
(2) The principle of apportionment of funds from public sources.
(3) The exercise of University powers by the affiliated Colleges.
(4) The composition of the general University Board.

III. (1) The Colleges affiliated under the University Board should be those which adopt a common curriculum, prescribed by a general University Board, which submit their students for simultaneous examination by Examiners appointed by such Board, and should have an adequate staff of Professors for giving instruction in the curriculum.

(2) The Senate would suggest that whatever funds the Legislature may see fit to set apart in aid of the Colleges affiliated by the University Act, exclusive of University College, should be divided into three equal parts, two of these to be divided equally amongst such Colleges, the other to be distributed in proportion to the beneficial results effected by such Colleges. It is to be understood that this suggestion is not intended to interfere with the endowment of University College, it being the opinion of the Senate that University College has a first claim to a fixed endowment amply sufficient to its support in its present state of efficiency; and that it should have the power to establish Faculties of Law and Medicine, with the same support which is granted to corresponding Faculties in the

other Colleges; and also that it should be placed as to University powers on a par with them.

(3) Such exercise should be limited to conferring degrees on such of their students as may have passed the prescribed examinations in the University of Upper Canada, except in the Faculty of Divinity.

(4) The number of the members of the Senate should be determined by the number of affiliated Colleges, one-third to be heads of such Colleges, one-third to be elected by the graduates of each College, and one-third to be appointed by the Provincial Government.

In connection with these answers the Senate would further beg to suggest that, in any new arrangement of the proposed University of Upper Canada, a Convocation should be created composed of the graduates of the Provincial University, with such powers as the Legislature may think fit to confer upon the said Convocation, and especially with that of the election of the Chancellor of the University.

———

COPY OF REPLY OF REVEREND DR. M'CAUL UPON AFFILIATION, ETC.

March 29, 1862.

SIR—In reply to the questions proposed to me by the Commissioners of inquiry relative to one University Board, and different systems of affiliation, I beg to state that I concur in the answers to these questions by the Senate of the University of Toronto.

I am, Sir, your obedient servant,
(Signed)   JOHN McCAUL.

D. BUCHAN, Esq., Secretary.

The above suggestions on academic points were unanimously assented to by the Senate, and Dr. McCAUL, as head of University College, gave his concurrence. The only financial point introduced into the replies of the Senate, and at the instance of those specially interested in the welfare of University College, was the following: " It is to be understood that this suggestion is not intended to interfere with the endowment of University College, it being the opinion of the Senate that University College has a first claim to a fixed endowment amply sufficient to its support in its present state of efficiency." This clause did not express any opinion as to the mode in which the surplus was to be applied—the act of 1853 having already determined that point.

The report of the Commission also embraces a financial as well as academic scheme, but this is not founded on any suggestions of the academic bodies. It is founded on the Act of 1853, which provides that "any surplus of the said University funds remaining at the end of any year, after defraying the expenses payable out of the same, shall constitute a fund to be from time to time payable, appropriated by Parliament for academic education in Upper Canada." The Commissioners refrained from putting any questions to the various Colleges in reference to the disposal of this surplus; they acted on their own responsibility, and made such proposals as the act of 1853 warranted. We have thus in the report an academic scheme emanating from the academic bodies, and a financial one emanating from the Commissioners themselves; and it is important, in the understanding of the question, that the two schemes should be conceived of as distinct. The financial scheme may prove to be impracticable, while the academic may still claim our support. And if a system of higher education be adopted unanimously by the academic bodies, we have reason to hope that adequate public support shall be secured by Parliament, though not in the precise manner suggested by the Commissioners.

At a recent meeting of the Senate of Toronto, the Commissioners' report was discussed, and a resolution was moved, the object of which was to withdraw the assent to the academic scheme which the Senate had previously given. After long discussion, in which the distinction between the financial and academic schemes was clearly pointed out, an amendment was unanimously carried leaving the academic scheme untouched, but affirming that in that scheme there was no sanction given to any plan of partitioning the revenues of the University. This was assented to by all, as it was clearly understood that the scheme of the Senate was purely academic, and that the proposed plan of apportioning the surplus emanated entirely from the Commissioners themselves. Another resolution was carried by a majority disapproving of the financial plan of the Commissioners. This, from the present constitution of the Senate, was to be looked for, and it was never anticipated that the Senate should approve of any such plan. The position of the question now is, that there is still the same unanimity as to the academic scheme; and this is the real point at issue, for sooner or later the financial question must be subordinated to what is best for the educational interests of the country. The settlement of the question has hitherto been retarded by basing it on financial grounds. There is more probability of a speedy settlement by first determining what academic scheme is best for the country, assured that the spread of enlightenment and a sense of justice will lead Parliament to provide adequate support for such scheme.

While the College aims at affording to the youth of Canada generally an academic education in the various faculties, it is always steadily kept in view that the special object of the Institution is to prepare ministers for the church with which it is closely connected, and that facilities are afforded other students only in as far as is compatible with this object. It is very important that the youth who are to form the future ministers of the church should, during the Arts as well as the Theological course, be surrounded with healthful religious influence. This is the ground on which the church maintains an Arts faculty, instead of requiring her students to study at Universities where no religious guarantee is afforded. The prosperity of the College will depend mainly on the warm interest taken in its welfare by the ministers and members of the church; and the Trustees again solicit a continuance of that interest, assured that by the blessing of God and the hearty support of the church, the institution will prove eminently successful in diffusing learning and promoting the cause of religion in Canada.

By order of the Board of Trustees.

W. IRELAND,
Secretary to the Board.

Kingston, 20th May, 1863.

GENERAL STATEMENT QUEEN'S

	$ c.	$ c.
Royal Charter		3107 37
Apparatus	3611 12	.
Library	3341 19	
Furniture, etc.	1416 09	
		8368 40
Bank Stock, 320 shares of Commercial Bank	32000 00	

Lands, viz :

16½ acres, Kingston, @ $800... ... ...$13200 00			
100 " S. ½ lot 25, 2nd con. Manvers ... 300 00			
100 " N. ½ " 19, 12th " Portland ... 300 00			
64 " rear " 4, 4th " S. Crosby ... 192 00			
100 " N. ½ " 19, 2nd " Marmora ... 300 00			
100 " E. ½ " 21, 11th " Belmont ... 300 00			
100 " N. ½ " 10, 9th " Tiny ... 300 00			
200 " " 12, 15th " Orillia, N.D., 600 00			
100 " S.E.½" 10, 12th " Sunnidale ... 300 00			
200 " " 15, 10th " " ... 600 00			
100 " E. ½ " 11, 1st " Plympton ... 300 00			
Lot 4, S. side Hannah street, Hamilton ... 100 00			

16792 00

Bonds and Mortgages, viz :

A. J. Macdonell (3) $4586 55
Rice Lewis (5)... ... ... 4800 00
D. McMillan 150 00

9536 55

Queen's College School and lot	1149 54	
Buildings and grounds of College	35701 89	
		95179 98
Toronto Bursary Stock, 7 shares and prem., Com'l Bank,	785 20	
Kingston do. 10 do. do. do.	1113 00	
		1898 20
Observatory		322 84

Commercial Bank, viz :

Endowment Funds deposited there $1600 00
Reinvestment do. do. 4000 00
Bursary do. do. 81 63
Scholarships do. do. 160 00
Ordinary do. do. 1648 03

7489 66

$116366 45

11

COLLEGE, 10th APRIL, 1863.

	$ c.	$ c.
Toronto Scholarship Endowment...	800 00	
Kingston do. do.	1113 00	
Prince of Wales do.	800 00	
Mowat do. do.	-800 00	
		3513 00
Campbell Scholarship	80 00	
Watkins do.	80 00	
Bursary account balance	81 63	
		241 63
Profit and Loss account		108018 89
Private Accounts, viz :		
Principal Leitch	2437 93	
Prof. Williamson	270 00	
" Mowat...	350 00	
" Weir	350 00	
" Lawson	350 00	
" Murray	750 00	
Librarian	80 00	
Prof. Dickson	5 00	
		4592 93

$116366 45

ANDREW DRUMMOND,
Treasurer.

Queen's University and College, Kingston, 10th April, 1862.
April 27th, 1863—Accounts audited and vouchers compared and found correct. GEO. DAVIDSON.

ABSTRACT STATEMENT SHOWING RECEIPTS AND

		$	c.
Balance on hand, 9th April, 1862, in Commercial Bank, per statement of that date		6692	22
To special receipts, viz :			
Account Mortgages	$500 00		
" Medical Faculty	1181 00		
Bursary account	910 28		
Account Observatory	504 87		
Campbell and Watkins' scholarships, $80 each... ...	160 00		
		3256	15
To ordinary receipts, viz :			
Government grant	5000 00		
Clergy Reserve Fund	2000 00		
Colonial Committee, Church of Scotland... ...	1470 00		
Interest, dividends, &c.	2950 11		
Fees, matriculation and class	748 00		
		12168	11

$22116 48

April 27th, 1863—Accounts audited and vouchers compared and found correct.
GEO. DAVIDSON.

DISBURSEMENTS, 9th APRIL, 1862, TO 10th APRIL, 1863.

By unpaid balances of private accounts, per statement of 9th April, 1862, since paid		3882 53
By special disbursements, viz:		
Account College buildings and ground	240 50	
Extra—ordinary proportion of travelling expenses of non-resident Trustees attending special meetings, and of Prof. Murray from Scotland...	300 00	
Bursaries to date, per separate account	1234 00	
Medical Faculty do.	1263 81	
Observatory	182 45	
		3220 76
By ordinary disbursements, viz:		
Principal, 12 months to 1st October, 1863 ...$2400 00		
Professors Williamson, Weir, and Mowat, 12 months to 1st October, 1863 ... ... 4500 00		
Rev. Dr. George, to 1st October, 1862... ... 750 00		
Prof. Lawson, 12 months to 1st October, 1863, 1100 00		
do. amount short of fees guaranteed 1861-2, $98; 1862-3, $252 ... ... 350 00		
Prof. Murray, 11 months to 1st October, 1863, 1341 67		
Secretary, to 1st March, 1863 ... ... 200 00		
Librarian, one year to 1st May, 1863 ... ... 80 00		
Amanuensis for Principal 20 00		
Janitor to 1st April, 1863 ... ... 300 00		
11041 67		
Less proportion Chemical Chair charged Medical Faculty above 500 00		
	10541 67	
Returned fees, students for ministry	16 00	
Advertising, printing account, stationery, &c., ...	343 40	
Miscellaneous expenses, viz:		
Fuel and light 122 48		
Sundry accounts for maintenance of property, 136 01		
	258 49	
Paid for postages $37 99, taxes $107 54	145 53	
" Insurance	195 25	
" Apparatus...	48 20	
" Books	153 21	
" Furniture	35 86	
Proportion of travelling expenses of non-resident Trustees,	78 85	
Scholarships Grammar School	300 00	
		12116 46
		19219 75
Deduct amount of unpaid private accounts, per general statement of this date		4592 93
		14626 82
Balance per general statement :—Com'l Bank deposited,		7489 66
		$22116 48

ANDREW DRUMMOND, Treasurer.
Queen's University and College, Kingston, 10th April, 1863.

Dr.   COMMERCIAL BANK OF CANADA.

1862.			$	c.
April 9,	To balance		6687	98
12,	" Students' Miss'y Assoc. University St. Andrews, £10		48	67
26,	" St. Andrew's Ch. Montreal Scholarship		64	00
May 5,	" Aberdeen Missionary Association £7		34	06
	" Cash deposited		12	00
15,	" Rev. J. Cook, balance of Quebec Bursary ...	...	31	50
June 14,	" Grant from Colonial Committee, £300 @ 10¼	...	1470	00
"	" do from Bursary, £50	...	245	00
"	" Fees Prof. Williamson	...	144	00
26,	" Account Mitchell's mortgage	...	65	00
July 4,	" Clergy Reserve Grant	...	1000	00
	" Government Grant	...	5000	00
	" Medical Faculty...	...	1000	00
	" Observatory	...	500	00
	" Dividend 3½ p. c. Commercial Bank Stock ...	...	1120	00
	" do Bursary Stock	...	59	50
28,	" Mitchell mortgage and interest	...	65	00

Carried forward $17546 71

COMMERCIAL BANK OF CANADA. Cr.

1862.								$	c.
April 10,	By Cheque	760,	G. S. Hobart	...	...	...	...	6	86
12,	"	761,	J. May ...	...	...	...	...	75	00
	"	762,	J. M. Creighton...	...	...	...	...	6	50
14,	"	763,	Bursary account	...	...	...	...	60	00
17,	"	764,	Prof. Weir	...	...	...	...	200	00
19,	"	765,	Taxes	...	...	...	...	39	96
23,	"	766,	Bursaries	...	...	...	...	488	00
25,	"	767,	J. C. Smith	...	...	...	...	20	00
"	"	768,	Rev. D. Morrison	...	...	...	...	8	00
26,	"	769,	Alex. McLean ...	...	...	...	...	13	72
"	"	770,	Rev. Dr. Urquhart	...	...	...	...	6	50
"	"	771,	Taxes	...	...	...	...	57	58
"	"	772,	Observatory	...	...	...	...	11	89
28,	"	773,	Bursaries	...	...	...	...	96	00
"	"	774,	do.	...	...	...	...	20	00
May 2,	"	775,	W. Ferguson & Co.	...	...	...	...	15	17
3,	"	776,	J. M. Creighton...	...	...	...	...	17	00
"	"	777,	Prof. Williamson	..	...	...	...	40	00
7,	"	778,	Prof. Lawson ...	...	...	...	...	100	00
	"	779,	J. Cameron	...	...	...	...	20	00
8,	"	780,	Rev. A. Spence ...	...	...	...	...	23	62
	"	781,	Rev. D. Morrison	...	...	...	...	4	00
15,	"	782,	Taxes ...	...	...	...	...	10	00
	"	783,	A. McLean ...	...	...	...	...	13	86
16,	"	784,	Rev. Dr. Urquhart	...	...	...	...	6	25
	"	785,	Rev. A. Spence...	...	...	...	...	10	00
19,	"	786,	Rev. J. George ...	...	...	...	...	750	00
21,	"	787,	W. Ireland	...	...	...	...	67	21
	"	788,	Rev. Dr. Barclay	...	...	...	...	25	50
	"	789,	Principal Leitch	...	...	...	...	1200	00
	"	790,	Presbyterian	...	...	...	...	6	00
27,	"	791,	J. Cormack ...	...	...	...	...	35	00
"	"	792,	Prof. Williamson	...	...	...	...	80	00
30,	"	793,	Librarian ...	...	...	...	...	80	00
June 12,	"	794,	Rev. Dr. Urquhart	...	...	...	...	6	50
16,	"	795,	Rev. D. Morrison	...	...	...	...	4	00
17,	"	796,	Prof. Williamson	...	...	...	...	230	00
19,	"	797,	Principal Leitch,	...	...	...	...	120	00
24,	"	798,	J. Cormack ...	...	...	...	...	6	38
30,	"	799,	Prof. Weir ...	...	...	...	...	175	00
July 1,	"	800,	Prof. Mowat, ...	...	...	...	...	375	00
4,	"	801,	T. W. Robison ...	...	...	...	...	27	70
10,	"	802,	Royal Insurance Co.	...	...	...	...	37	50
"	"	803,	Prof. Lawson ...	...	...	...	...	268	61
11,	"	804,	J. Cormack ...	...	...	...	...	40	00
14,	"	805,	R. M. Horsey ...	...	...	...	...	17	78
Aug. 13,	"	806,	J. Rowlands ...	...	...	...	...	6	30
	"	807,	do. ...	...	...	...	...	161	29

Carried forward $5099 68

DR.   **COMMERCIAL BANK OF CANADA.**

1862.						$	c.
	Brought forward				...17546	71
Aug. 25,	To Campbell scholarship					80	00
	" Bursary from Brockville congregation					20	00
Nov. 20,	" Rice Lewis, int. on mortgages $144, less bank com.,					143	64
26,	" Balance of Caldwell's mortgage					416	00
28,	" Account of fees deposited per W. Ireland					316	00
Dec. 16,	" do. do.					50	00
20,	" do. do.					84	00
27,	" Bursary, H. Allan					50	00
1863.							
Jan'y 3,	" Clergy Reserve Fund					1000	00
"	" Dividend 3½ Commercial Bank stock...					1120	00
" "	do. Kingston Bursary Fund					35	00
	do. Toronto do.					24	50

Carried forward $20885 85

COMMERCIAL BANK OF CANADA. Cr.

								$	c.
1862.									
	Brought forward		...	...	...	...	...	5089	68
Aug. 14,	By Cheque	808,	Advertising	...	...	...	...	158	96
15,	"	809,	Observatory	...	...	...	...	7	00
22,	"	810,	W. Ferguson & Co.	...	...	...	6	10
	"	811,	W. Ferguson & Co.	...	...	...	10	09
23,	"	812,	Thos. McAuley...	...	...	...	14	85
	"	813,	J. Cormack	...	...	...	...	35	00
Sept. 1,	"	814,	W. Ireland	..	...	...	...	54	40
8,	"	815,	Front garden	...	...	...	...	8	62
	"	816,	G. M. Wilkinson	...	...	...	4	65
Oct. 1,	"	817,	Prof. Mowat	...	...	...	...	500	00
"	"	818,	Prof. Lawson	...	...	...	...	400	00
"	"	819,	Prof. Weir	...	...	...	...	400	00
2,	"	820,	Prof. Williamson	...	...	...	750	00
"	"	821,	Prof. Mowat	...	...	...	...	250	00
"	"	822,	Tieman's account	...	...	...	49	30
4,	"	823,	M. Judge	...	...	...	...	38	50
6,	"	824,	A. McLennan	...	...	...	...	16	00
"	"	825,	Dr. Dickson	...	...	...	...	11	00
9,	"	826,	J. Cormack	...	...	...	...	40	00
"	"	827,	do.	...	...	...	...	12	25
10,	"	828,	Rev. Dr. Urquhart	...	...	...	6	00
"	"	829,	M. Kelligher	...	...	...	...	140	40
"	"	830,	Judge Logie	...	...	...	...	10	00
14,	"	831,	J. B. Mowat	...	...	...	...	3	50
25,	"	832,	Prof. Weir	...	...	...	...	350	00
Nov. 1,	"	833,	E. J. Barker	...	...	...	...	15	00
10,	"	834,	Rev. J. McMorine	...	...	...	10	00
11,	"	835,	Liverpool and London Ins. Co.		...	30	00
19,	"	836,	Skinner & Co. ...	...	...	...	16	00
"	"	837,	J. M. Creighton	...	...	...	8	50
22,	"	838,	E. J. Barker	...	...	...	...	4	74
26,	"	839,	J. Cormack	...	...	...	...	35	00
27,	"	840,	Bursary ...	...	...	...	...	40	00
Dec. 1,	"	841,	W. Ireland	...	...	...	...	59	46
"	"	842,	Prof. Murray	...	...	...	...	400	00
"	"	843,	Principal Leitch	...	...	...	1000	00
6,	"	844,	Cataraque Cemetery Co.	...	...	63	00
8,	"	845,	Royal Ins. Co. ...	...	...	...	30	25
16,	"	846,	G. S. Hobart	...	...	...	...	49	57
"	"	847,	Bursaries	...	...	...	...	120	00
"	"	848,	do.	...	...	...	...	40	00
"	"	849,	do.	...	...	...	...	100	00
22,	"	850,	do.	...	...	...	...	40	00
23,	"	851,	Dr. Lavell	...	...	...	...	11	80
26,	"	852,	Bursary ...	...	...	...	...	25	00
"	"	853,	do. ...	...	...	...	...	20	00
27,	"	854,	J. & D. Cunningham	...	...	...	51	80

Carried forward...   ...   .$ 10536 42

_{DR.}   **COMMERCIAL BANK OF CANADA.**

1863.			$	c.
	Brought forward	..20885	85
Jan.	20,	To Deposited per W. Ireland, acc't fees	52	00
	23,	" 8 mos. rent Q. C. School	66	66
		" Int. on acc't current in bank Jan. to 31st Dec., 1862	309	81
Feb.	17,	" J. Watkins' scholarship	80	00
	"	" Bursary Kingston congregation	28	60
		" W. Ireland, acc't fees	40	00
	27,	" Cash acc't deposited	12	00
		" Bursary, St. Andrews Ch., Montreal...	64	00
		" Perth congregation	20	60
		" Spencerville do.	16	00

Carried forward $21575 52

COMMERCIAL BANK OF CANADA. CR.

1862.					$	c.
	Brought forward	... ...		..10536	42
Dec. 27,	By Cheque 855,	Grammar School scholarship ...	...	300	00
29,	"	856, Bursary	...	20	00
"	"	857, Dr. Lavell	...	17	18
1863.					
Jan'y 5,	"	858, J. Cormack	...	30	00
"	"	859, J. Cormack	...	10	00
"	"	860, Bursary	...	20	00
"	"	861, do.	...	40	00
8,	"	ꝰ62, Phœnix Ins. Co.	...	30	00
"	"	863, Bursary	...	20	00
"	"	864, A. McLean	..	8	40
27,	"	865, Rev. Dr. Urquhart	...	9	50
27,	"	866, W. Allan...	...	2	80
28,	"	867, Prof. Lawson	...	158	83
30,	"	868, Rev. D. Morrison	...	5	00
31,	"	869, A. Davidson	...	314	21
Feb'y 3,	"	870, A. Morris	...	14	50
6,	"	871, Chown & Cunningham... ...	...	23	15
16,	"	1, Prof. Lawson	...	65	00
17,	"	2, Appleton & Co.	...	8	40
"	"	3, Gas Company	...	4	00
"	"	4, J. Duff	...	25	63
"	"	5, Librarian	...	6	51
24,	"	6, J. Duff	...	16	88
25,	"	7, J. Cormack	...	35	00
"	"	8, Bursary	...	20	00
March 2,	"	9, W. Ireland	...	55	57
3,	"	10, Medical Janitor...	..	12	00
4,	"	11, J. M. Creighton...	...	17	00
5,	"	12, North British Ins. Co.... ...	...	67	50
11,	"	13, W. Hay	...	4	50
"	"	14, S. T. Drennan	...	30	00
"	"	15, Davidson & Doran	...	57	86
"	"	16, G. S. Hobart	...	19	36
"	"	17, W. Lightfoot	...	3	00
"	"	18, Fraser & George	...	3	65
"	"	19, T. W. Robison	...	20	06
"	"	20, Do.	...	46	23
"	"	21, R. M. Horsey	...	14	16
"	"	22, Moore & Skinner	...	13	68
"	"	23, W. C. Chewett & Co.	...	25	00
"	"	24, Fraser & George	...	6	00
"	"	25, Presbyterian	...	10	00
"	"	26, Prof. Lawson	...	230	28
17,	"	27, Prof. Murray	...	343	17
23,	"	28, Chas. Tanner	...	40	00
"	"	29, Armstrong & Co.	...	7	60
	Carried forward			...$12768	03

Dr. **COMMERCIAL BANK OF CANADA.**

1863.							$	c.
	Brought forward	....	...	...	...	...	...21575	52
M'ch 9,	To Cornwall congregation ...		...	...	...	...	40	00
11,	" W. Ireland, account fees		...	...	...	...	68	00
	" Cheque 14, Drennan, contra cancelled			...		...	30	00
21,	" Anonymous French Mission Bursary, for Chas. Tanner,						40	00
27,	" Cash account deposited...		...	...	...	...	42	25
April 9,	" 6 mos. int., Rice Lewis, on mortgage...			...		...	144	00

$ 21939 77

1863.

April 10, To balance, as per general statement $7489 77

April 27th, 1863—Compared with vouchers, audited and found correct.

GEO. DAVIDSON.

COMMERCIAL BANK OF CANADA. Cr.

1863.									$	c.
	Brought forward		...	...	...	...	...	...	...12768	03
M'ch 23,	By Cheque	30,	R. Hall ...	...	...	...	...	12	00
"	"	31,	Prof. Williamson		...	...	...	40	20
"	"	32,	John Duff	...	...	...	...	35	00
April 2,	"	33,	Prof. Williamson		...	...	...	240	00
4,	"	34,	Prof. Mowat	...	...	...	...	400	00
"	"	35,	" Williamson		...	...	...	250	00
"	"	36,	" Weir	...	...	...	...	400	00
"	"	37,	" Lawson	...	...	...	...	200	00
8,	"	38,	R. M. Horsey	...	...	...	...	42	49
"	"	39,	J. Cormack	...	...	...	...	40	00
10,	"	40,	Bursary ...	...	...	...	...	20	00
"	"	41,	Cash ...	...	...	...	...	2	04
			Comm'n on Rice Lewis			...	...		35
			Balance ...	...	...	...	...	7489	66
								$ 21939	77

Queen's University and College, Kingston, 10th April, 1863.

ANDREW DRUMMOND, Treasurer.

DR.   **TEMPORARY CASH ACCOUNT.**

1862.	Balance ... ... $	4 24
April 25,	To Observatory donation, 1 sovereign	4 87
28,	" Additional matriculation fees, Prof. Weir	4 00
May 7,	" Bursary, Belleville congregation	10 00
15,	" do. Milton do.	3 10
June 26,	" Mitchell's mortgage	65 00
Oct. 1,	" Bursary. Brockville congregation	20 00
Dec. 10,	" Fees from T. F. Harkness	50 00
1863.		
Jan. 30,	" Bursary, anonymous, per A. Morris	2 00
Feb. 16,	" " Arnprior congregation	5 00
	" Watkins' scholarship	80 00
17,	" Valcartier congregation Bursary	2 00
M'ch 27,	" Bursary, Ross and Westmeath congregation	5 00
	" do. St. Andrew's Church, Hamilton	43 25
April 10,	" Cheque 41, Commercial Bank	2 04

$ 300 50

TEMPORARY CASH ACCOUNT. Cr.

1862.		
May 5,	By Commercial Bank, deposited ... ...$	12 00
27,	" Disbursements, per Janitor's account	1 90
28,	" Postages	40
June 28,	" Deposited Commercial Bank	65 00
July 19,	" Paid laborer 7 days, man in front grounds	5 25
31,	" Postages	20
Aug. 28,	" A. & S. Chown's account	50
Oct. 28,	" Commercial Bank, deposited	20 00
Dec. 16,	" do. do. do.	50 00
1863.		
Feb. 17,	" do. do. do.	80 00
"	" Postage stamps	2 00
27,	" Commercial Bank	12 00
M'ch 21,	" Observatory, Cunningham's account	1 25
28,	" Commercial Bank, deposited	42 25
	" M. Gill's account, crapes for mourning, Dr. Machar's funeral	3 75
April 7,	" Library, McKenzie's Life	2 50
	" Medical Faculty, paid for rubbers	1 50
		$ 300 50

Queen's University and College, Kingston, 10th April, 1863.

ANDREW DRUMMOND, Treasurer.

DR.   **PROFIT AND LOSS ACCOUNT.**

To Miscellaneous expenses, transferred	...	...	...	...	$	258 49
" Postage,	do.	...	...	...	...	37 99
" Travelling expenses,	do.	...	...	...	...	378 85
" Returned fees,	do.	...	...	...	...	16 00
" Taxes,	do.	...	...	...	...	107 54
" Insurance,	do.	...	...	...	...	195 25
" Advertising and Printing,	do.	...	...	...	...	343 40
" Scholarships, Gram. School,	do.	...	...	...	...	300 00
" Salaries,	do.	...	...	...	...	10541 67
" Medical Department, balance, do.	...	...	...	...		239 54
	Balance	...	...	...	...	108018 89
						$120437 62

PROFIT AND LOSS ACCOUNT. Cr.

1862.
April 19, By balance 9th April, 1862 ... ...$108269 51
    10, " Government grant 5000 00
        " Clergy Reserve do. 2000 00
        " Colonial Committee, Church of Scotland... ... 1470 00
        " Interest account 2950 11
        " Fees account 748 00

$120437 62

1863.
April 10, By balance $108018 89

Dr.   **BURSARY ACCOUNT.**

1862.									$	c.
April		To Printing Circulars	...	...	...	...	...	...	3	50
	14,	Paid J. Goodwell	...	...	...	...	...	...	20	00
		" do.	...	...	...	...	...	...	20	00
		" A. Hunter	...	...	...	...	...	...	20	00
	23,	" L. McAlister	...	...	...	...	...	...	12	00
		" Elias Mullen	...	...	...	...	...	...	20	00
		" W. Ross	...	...	...	...	...	...	20	00
		" R. Jardine	...	...	...	...	...	...	20	00
		" J. B. Mullen	...	...	...	...	...	...	20	00
		" J. McCaul	...	...	...	...	...	...	20	00
		" W. Hamilton	...	...	...	...	...	...	20	00
		" G. Milligan	...	...	...	...	...	...	20	00
		" C. J. Cameron	...	...	...	...	...	...	40	00
		" W. McGeachy	...	...	...	...	...	...	60	00
		" J. R. Ross	...	...	...	...	...	...	36	00
		" A. Hunter	...	...	...	...	...	...	20	00
		" D. J. McLean	...	...	...	...	...	...	20	00
		" W. McGeachy	...	...	...	...	...	...	20	00
		" A. Jamieson	...	...	...	...	...	...	20	00
		" J. C. Smith	...	...	...	...	...	...	20	00
		" Joshua Fraser	...	...	...	...	...	...	20	00
		" D. Ross	...	...	...	...	...	...	20	00
		" A. McBain	...	...	...	...	...	...	40	00
		" D. Ross	...	...	...	...	...	...	20	00
	28,	" Elias Mullen	...	...	...	...	...	...	20	00
		" H. Lamont	...	...	...	...	...	...	20	00
		" Donald Fraser	...	...	...	...	...	...	20	00
		" J. D. Robertson	...	...	...	...	...	...	56	00
Nov.	27,	" W. McGeachy	...	...	...	...	...	...	40	00
Dec.	18,	" D. Fraser	...	...	...	...	...	...	20	00
		" R. Jardine	...	...	...	...	...	...	20	00
		" A. Jamieson	...	...	...	...	...	...	20	00
		" H. Edmison	...	...	...	...	...	...	20	00
		" W. McLennan	...	...	...	...	...	...	20	00
		" A. G. McLean	...	...	...	...	...	...	20	00
	19,	" J. R. Ross	...	...	...	...	...	...	20	00
		" C. J. Cameron	...	...	...	...	...	...	20	00
	20,	" D. G. McKay	...	...	...	...	...	...	20	00
		" Alex. MacDonald	...	...	...	...	...	...	20	00
		" J. D. Robertson	...	...	...	...	...	...	20	00
		" Evan McAulay	...	...	...	...	...	...	20	00
		" James C. Smith	...	...	...	...	...	...	20	00
	22,	" Elias Mullen	...	...	...	...	...	...	20	00
		" Donald Macauley	...	...	...	...	...	...	20	00
	26,	" G. Milligan	..	...	...	...	...	...	25	00
		" James McCaul	...	...	...	...	...	...	20	00
	29,	" Donald Ross	...	...	...	...	...	...	20	00

Carried forward $1072 50

BURSARY ACCOUNT. Cr.

1862.		
April 9, By balance as per statement of date		$405 35
" St. Andrew's University Missionary Association, £10 stg.... ... ... $ 48 67		
" St. Andrew's Church, Montreal 64 00		
May 5, " Aberdeen Missionary Association, £7 stg. 34 06		
7, " Belleville Congregation 10 00		
15, " Milton do. 3 10		
" St. Andrew's Church, Quebec 50 00		
June 14, " Colonial Com. Church of Scotland, £50 stg. 245 00		
July 4, " Dividend on Toronto Endowment Stock ... 24 50		
" do. Kingston do. ... 35 00		
Oct. 1, " Collection St. John's Church, Brockville, for entrant in Divinity Class highest in Arts previous year 20 00		
Dec. 27, " Hugh Allan, bursary 50 00		
" Dividend Kingston Endowment Stock ... 35 00		
" do. Toronto do. ... 24 50		
1863.		
Jan. 30, By anonymous contribution 2 00		
Feb. 16, " Arnprior Congregation 5 00		
" Kingston do. 28 60		
" Valcartier do. 2 00		
27, " Montreal St. Andrew's Church 64 00		
" Perth Congregation 20 60		
" Spencerville do. 16 00		
" Anonymous contribution for a French Mission Bursary 40 00		
Mar. 9, " Cornwall Congregation 40 00		
27, " Congregation Ross and Westmeath ... 5 00		
" St. Andrew's Church, Hamilton 43 25		
		910 28

Carried forward $1315 63

D<small>R.</small>   **BURSARY ACCOUNT.**   .

1863.							$	c.
	Brought forward	...	...	...	...	...	...1072	50
Jan'y 5,	Paid G. A. Yeomans...	...	...	...	...	...	20	00
7,	" H. Lamont	...	...	...	...	...	 20	00
	" Joshua Fraser ...	...	...	...	...	...	20	00
8,	" Alex. Hunter	...	...	...	...	...	20	00
Feb. 25,	" W. Hamilton	...	...	...	...	...	20	00
	" Printing Circulars	...	...	...	...	...	1	50
Mar. 23,	" French Mission Bursary to Charles Tanner					...	40	00
April 10,	" A. Hunter	...	..	...	...	...	20	00
							$1234	00
	Balance	...	...	...	...	...	81	63
							$1315	63

BURSARY ACCOUNT. Cr.

Brought forward	$1315 63

	$1315 63
By balance	$81 63

Queen's University and College, Kingston, 10th April, 1862.

ANDREW DRUMMOND,
Treasurer.

NOTE.—See Supplementary Account, pages 34-5.

DR. **MEDICAL FACULTY.**

1862.	Balance		$ 156 73
July	To Peabody's account	5 00	
	" Horsey's do.	17 78	
	" J. Lovell's do.	3 00	
	" G. M. Wilkinson	4 65	
	" Chown & Cunningham	5 83	
	" T. W. Robison's account	27 70	
	" W. Ferguson & Co.	6 10	
	" G. S. Hobart	7 73	
Aug.	" Advertising, Session 1862–3	58 96	
Oct. 3,	" Draft on N.Y. to pay Tieman & Co.'s acc't. $58, for apparatus	49 30	
	" M. Judge's account, engraving Professor's plates for class cards	38 50	
	" M. Judge, re-engraving plate	8 00	
	" Express charge on apparatus	3 00	
	" Proportion of wood, say 24 cords	64 80	
	" Hobart's account for alcohol, ...	6 86	
	" do. for jars, etc.	31 81	
Dec. 6,	" Lots 36 and 37, Cataraque Cemetery ...	63 80	
23,	" Dr. Lavell, for instruments...	11 80	
1863.			
Jan'y	" do. for drawings, etc.	17 18	
"	" W. Allen's account	2 80	
Feb. 17,	" 10¼ cords of wood	25 63	
M'ch 3,	" R. Hall, Janitor, for February	12 00	
"	" H. Skinner's account	13 68	
"	" Fraser & George, saw	6 00	
"	" Chewett, diplomas	25 00	
"	" Hobart, balance of account...	16 36	
"	" Salary of Sec'y and Janitor, and sundry acc'ts, as per statement of Secretary, Prof. Lawson	148 03	
	" T. W. Robison's account	46 23	
	" J. Duff, 6¾ cords of wood	16 88	
	" R. M. Horsey, balance	6 70	
	" Proportion of grant for the Chemical Chair	500 00	
M'ch 27,	" 1 mo. wages paid Janitor	12 00	
April 7,	" ½ doz. rubbers	1 50	
		1263 81	
			$1420 54

MEDICAL FACULTY. CR.

1862.			
July 4	By Government grant $1000	00
1863.			
March	" Graduation fees, per account of Secretary... ... 181	00
		$1181	00
	Balance transferred to profit and loss, to clear off		
	for new statutes 239	54

$1420 54

Dr.   **OBSERVATORY ACCOUNT.**

		$	c.
1862.			
	To Balance 9th April	645	26
April 26,	" J. Rowlands, advertising ...$11 89		
Aug. 15,	" Sundry disbursements per Prof. Williamson, 7 00		
	" Advertising ... 3 93		
Nov. 15,	" Davidson & Doran's account for work and iron about Observatory ... 40 00		
1863.			
Jan. 27,	" Sundry tables, stands, seats, etc., per acc't A. Davidson ... 72 92		
	" Blank books, per acc't. T. W. Robison ... 2 50		
	" G. S. Hobart's acc't. lamps ... 3 00		
	" Chown & Cunningham's acc't. for stove, etc., 23 15		
	" W. Lightfoot's acc't. for 250 circulars ... 3 00		
Feb. 17,	" Coal and gas ... 4 00		
M'ch 21,	" Paid Cunningham, repairing diagrams ... 1 25		
	" Armstrong & Benedict's acc't... 7 60		
April 7,	" Lantern, postages, etc., per Prof. Williamson, 2 00		
		182	45
		$ 827	71
	To balance ... ...$ 322 84		

OBSERVATORY ACCOUNT. Cʀ.

1862.		$	c.	$	c.
April 28,	By Donation from a friend, per Dr. Yates, 1 sov.,	4	87,		
July 4,	" Government grant 500	00			
				504	87
	" Balance.			322	84

$ 827 71

Dr.   **BURSARY ACCOUNT, SUPPLEMENTARY.**

1863.						$	c.
April 27,	To paid	Donald Fraser				20	00
	"	J. Goodwell $20 and $20				40	00
28,	"	C. J. Cameron, bal. of Montreal St. Andrew's					
		Ch. scholarship				44	00
29,	"	Henry Edmison				20	00
	"	J. Ross				40	00
	"	A. G. McBean				60	00
30,	"	R. Jardine				60	00
	"	A. Jamieson				20	00
	"	A. McGregor				25	00
	"	D. McAulay...				20	00
	"	Evan McAulay				20	00
	"	H. Lamont				20	00
	"	J. C. Smith				20	00
	"	Joshua Fraser				20	00
	"	Jas. McCaul				20	00
May 1,	"	Wm. Hamilton				20	00
	"	Elias Mullen				20	00
	"	W. McLennan				20	00
2,	"	Geo. Milligan				25	00
	"	Alex. McDonald				20	00
5,	"	D. McDonald				40	00
	"	Donald Ross...				20	00
						$614	00

May 27, To uncovered balance this date $248 04

BURSARY ACCOUNT, SUPPLEMENTARY. Cʀ.

1863.			$	c.
April 10,	By Balance this date		81	63
23,	" Missionary Association, University of St. Andrews, £7 10s. stg.		36	50
25,	" Collection, Milton congregation		2	00
May 20,	" do. Pakenham do.		2	50
27,	" Colonial Committee Church Scotland, £50 stg. ...		243	33
	Balance		248	04

$614 00

ANDREW DRUMMOND, Treasurer.

STUDENTS IN MEDICINE, SESSION 1862-3.

Agnew, John
Allen, Geo. C.
Anderson, Thos.
Armstrong, Alfred
Aylsworth, Arch'd K.
Beattie, Wm.
Beckett, James
Bell, Alexander
Bell, John
Bigham, John
Bigham, Hugh
Bray, John L.
Brownley, Charles
Bredin, Hawtrey
Campbell, Joseph
Chanonhouse, John
Coleman, Wm. F.
Comer, Alex. T. C.
Corbett, Henry
Darragh, Robert J.
Davidson, Myers
Deans, George
Dickson, John
Dunn, Andrew T.
Ellerbeck, Chas. H.
Elwell, W. D.
Fenwick, Thomas M.
Ferguson, E. G.
Ferguson, John A.
Ferguson, R. B.

Fortune, Lewis
Fox, Edward C.
Fralick, G. B.
Gleeson, James
Grasse, J. C.
Grasse, Sidney D.
Hickey, D. C.
Hoare, Walter W.
Horsey, Alfred J.
Howells, T. B.
Ingersoll, I. F.
Irwin, C. A.
Kertland, Edward H.
Kincaid, Robert
Maiden, W. P.
Malloch, A. E.
Massie, John
Millener, W. S.
Monro, John C.
Moore, Andrew
Morden, James B.
Muir, Thomas
McCammon, James
McIntyre, Duncan
McIntyre, John F.
McKee, Thomas
McLaren, Alex.
McLean, Thos. F.
Neish, James
Nesbitt, Edward

Newton, John
Nichol, James
Nugent, Robert J. S.
Oliver, A. S.
O'Conner, Roderick
Price, R. B.
Reeve, R. A.
Robb, James
Ross, Thomas K.
Rourke, Francis
Ruttan, Joseph B.
Searls, Abram W.
Selleck, John D.
Shirley, Jos. W.
Shurtliff, —   Camden.
Skinner, —
Sanders, —
Smith, John R.
Sullivan, Thomas
Taylor, James B.
Thornton, Wm. M.
Tossell, John
Tracy, Thomas B.
Wafer, Francis M.
Wartman, P. G.
Watson, Chas. V., M.D.
Weeks, Wm. James
Wilson, T. C.
Wilson, John A.
Yeomans, Horace P.

The following Students in the Faculty of Arts are studying with a view to the ministry of the Presbyterian Church of Canada, in connection with the Church of Scotland:

FIRST YEAR.

James Fraser,
James Gray,

Alex. McBean,
John R. Thomson,

Alex. McGregor.

SECOND YEAR.

Donald Fraser,
Wm. McLennan,

Daniel McGillivray,
Elias Mullan,

Charles Tanner,
Donald McAulay.

THIRD YEAR.

Wm. R. Bain,
Henry Edmison,
Alex. Jamieson,

Robert Jardine,
Evan McAulay,

George Thomson,
George A. Yeomans.

Statements and Treasurer's Accounts,

OF

The University of Queen's College,

KINGSTON.

––––––––––––

Printed by Order of the Board of Trustees.

ANNUAL REPORT

OF THE

Board of Trustees of Queen's College.

The near approach of the meeting of Synod, affords the Trustees another opportunity of placing before the Presbyterian Church of Canada in connection with the Church of Scotland a statement of the affairs of this University, together with full information in regard to its present position. Although open to and entered by students of all denominations, Queen's College has peculiar claims upon the sympathies and aid of all in this Province who claim connection with the Church of Scotland, as the training Institution for the Ministry of that Church, with its Theological and Arts Faculties in large measure supported by Church Funds, and also as, under the wise provisions of the Royal Charter, controlled by Trustees who are Ministers or members of the same Church.

The number of students in the various Faculties was as follows at the close of the College Session:—

Arts	39
Theology	22
Medicine	85
Law	7
	153

It is with much satisfaction that the Trustees are again able to report an increase to the number of students in the Theological Hall, 22 forming the largest class ever enrolled, and being an increase of five over last year. In view of the many vacant stations of our Church, and of the large districts where the Presbyterian population attached to her communion are as yet unprovided for, the growth of this department of Queen's College gives it stronger claims upon the attention of the Synod. The number of students in the Arts Faculty who have announced their intention to study for the Ministry is 19, so that the Queen's College is now preparing 41 for the sacred office.

The plan mentioned in last Report of affording practical training for the pastoral office by employing the senior Theological students in Missionary and Sabbath School duty has been continued, and the success with which it has been attended has been very encouraging. Two Mission stations, and the Kingston Hospital, Gaol, and House of Industry, have thus been regularly supplied on Sabbath with religious services, chiefly conducted by students under the supervision of the Principal, and at four Sabbath Schools they are employed in the work of instruction. This training is found by the students to be of great service, and is, at the same time, regarded by them as a labor of love in which they can readily engage without injury to their course of study during the week. Mr. JAMES B. MULLEN is entitled to special mention for the efficient manner in which he has aided the Principal to carry on the system thus successfully introduced.

A new exercise in pulpit elocution has been tried, and which promises satisfactory results. The Theological students in rotation are called upon to deliver short discourses *memoriter* in the Convocation Hall, which are heard by the Professors, and the delivery is then criticised by them. This exercise is in addition to the regular discourses delivered in the classroom; and during the weekly hour, thus occupied, these students have a valuable opportunity afforded to them of employing their oratorical powers, and of benefiting by the experienced advice of their instructors. Defects of delivery or of style uncorrected in youth may mar the future success of a Minister, and greatly detract from his usefulness. It is hoped that ere long arrangements may be made for the delivery of regular lectures in Queen's College on Rhetoric and Elocution, but in meanwhile the plan thus adopted may be considered as a valuable addition to the course of instruction. The peculiar circumstances of Canada require that special attention should be paid to the mode of securing an effective delivery. In more settled states of society, where associations and habits are fixed and permanent, a Minister may prove eminently useful though his pulpit talents are of an inferior order; but in a new country it is essential that he be an effective speaker to gather a large congregation around him. It is true that in most localities there are settlers who are ardently attached to the Church of Scotland, and who cling to her services under every disadvantage; yet there are but few districts where a large congregation can be formed without drawing in many who have no such ties, and these will, at first, be attracted chiefly by the personal gifts of the

The Faculty of Law has been sustained with considerable success, and the progress made by the students during the Session was such as to draw forth the highest commendation from their Professors. So long, however, as the lectures in this Faculty are not regarded as a substitute for the keeping of Terms at Osgoode Hall, the department will labor under a great disadvantage. Representations having been made to many gentlemen of eminence in the legal profession with favorable results, the College has memorialized the Law Society on the subject. Should the desired boon be granted, the legal education of a student will be completed without the expense and inconvenience of going to Toronto; and there is the more hope of such a concession, as it is admitted that the longer attendance and steadier application of students under the Law Faculty enable them to acquire a much larger amount of legal knowledge than is possible during the short and broken periods spent in Toronto in keeping term.

Several important changes in the Medical Faculty will contribute greatly to its efficiency and usefulness. Through the munificence of a citizen of Kingston, JOHN WATKINS, Esq., who has given £1000 cy. to add a wing to the Kingston Hospital, a spacious Clinical Lecture Room and Operating Theatre will be enjoyed by this Institution. The want of such accommodation has long been felt as a serious drawback to the Hospital practice of students. Some change in the existing laws of the Province relating to the medical profession is greatly needed, and it is hoped that ere long the powers of the various bodies entitled to grant medical degrees, and also the course of study and examination standards may be better defined. This object might be accomplished, as in England, by a Medical Council established for the purpose, or by incorporating the Medical Faculties with the University system of Upper Canada. The importance of such a change to the medical profession, and also to the whole Province, cannot be doubted, and it is earnestly hoped that the whole subject may ere long receive favorable attention on the part of Government or of the Legislature.

The state of the Bursary scheme will be seen from the accounts in the appendix, and the Trustees have only to add that the funds at their disposal have been very limited, and quite inadequate to meet the wants of deserving young men preparing for the Ministry. As has been already stated, all funds in aid of this scheme received from Church collections, and also such donations from private individuals as may be given with that view, are specially reserved for the benefit of young men who have declared their intention to enter the Ministry. The Trustees have pleasure in adding that they are yearly able to increase the number of competition scholarships open to all students, through the wise liberality of many friends of the Church and College, and that such rewards are not only a great stimulus in the pursuit of learning, but also afford welcome aid to the meritorious student in meeting his necessary expenses.

An important step, which may be expected to exercise a beneficial influence upon the College, was lately taken in establishing a connection between the magnificent Common School system of Upper Canada with the Grammar School of Kingston, now affiliated to Queen's College. A considerable number of Scholarships are offered for competition among boys in the Kingston Common Schools, tenable during their Grammar School course, and several larger Scholarships have been endowed by private individuals from the Grammar Schools of the district to the College. This link has long been wanting, and the regular gradation from the lower education to the higher having been established, it is believed that a much larger proportion of our Canadian youth may be expected to seek the advantage of University training than has hitherto been the case. With the view of aiding this movement, and also of improving both schools, the College Preparatory School was amalgamated with the Kingston Grammar School, the practical control of the latter having been secured to the College. The result so far has been most encouraging. A full and accomplished staff of masters have been secured, and the increase in the number of boys during the very short period which has intervened since the change was effected justifies the expectation that this important feeder to the College will occupy a high osi ion among the educational institutions of Upper Canada. t

The Botanical and Astronomical Societies connected with Queen's College have prospered during the past Session, and their contributions to the important sciences which they represent in Canada have been of great value. A portion of the College grounds having been laid out as a Botanical Garden, a fine collection of plants was obtained during the autumn; and the Museum is also enriched by a growing collection of botanical specimens. The public lectures given by the Principal in connection with the Astronomical Society were attended by crowded audiences, and the interest felt in the Society is such as to lead to the confident expectation that the necessary expensive instruments required by the Kingston Observatory will ere long be secured. It must be a subject of no small gratification to the friends of Queen's College to find that she is able, through her learned Principal and Professors, to render such important services to the cause of science, without in any way trenching upon her limited means, or interferiug with the course of Collegiate instruction; and the position thus taken cannot fail to raise the character and reputation of the University not only in Canada but also in Europe.

The College Library has received some valuable additions during the past year, and handsome donations of Books have been received from Professor STEVENSON, Convener of the Colonial Committee of the Church of Scotland; Principal LEITCH; ALEX. MORRIS, Esq., M.P.P.; President NELLES, of Victoria College; and others. The general condition of the Library, however, is still far from satisfactory, the number of volumes being only about 4000, with many blanks to be filled up before it can meet the wants of Professors or Students.

The movement made during the past year towards a satisfactory settlement of the long vexed University question in Upper Canada is of very great importance to Queen's College. The misappropriation and wasteful expenditure of the munificent endowment obviously intended for the benefit of University education generally, instead of, as has been practically the case, for the fostering of one College at Toronto to the exclusion of all others, is a fact which has long been anxiously considered by the Trustees. They feel, however, that another question of even greater importance is involved, viz. the elevation and permanence of the University system of Upper Canada. Until the result of the labors of the Government Commission now sitting are laid before Parliament, the effect of this movement cannot be anticipated; but all legislation on the subject will be carefully watched by the Trustees. In order to ascertain the views of other Universities upon this important question, and thus pave the way for its satisfactory settlement, the Principal spent some time in Toronto during the past winter, and met with gratifying success in his endeavors to promote unity of action among the bodies most deeply interested. The Trustees take this opportunity of acknowledging their sense of his valuable services, not only to Queen's College, but also to the cause of University education in this matter; and they cannot better explain the course taken than by giving the following extract from the Principal's able address at the close of the College Session :—

"An attempt was made last winter, by friendly conferences, to come to some understanding as to a plan which might be satisfactory to the various Universities, and, at the same time, effectually promote the cause of higher education. This attempt has been crowned with the most satisfactory success. It was found, in conference, that Universities which by political necessities had been ranged in hostile array against each other, were really one in spirit and in aim—that there was but one universal feeling to do something to raise the character of University education. The grand defect of the present system of affiliation, is that every temptation is presented to lower the standard of education. The kind of rivalry that exists, at present, is one that necessarily tends towards depression. Besides, the resources of the country are dissipated in fragmentary efforts instead of being applied to the maintenance of one grand consistent and national scheme in which the whole country might be embraced. The problem was simply to establish a system which would develope a rivalry tending to the elevation, instead of the lowering of the standard, and to unite the whole into one great national institution. After much consultation a plan was devised which received the most gratifying approval from all the parties chiefly interested in this question. The main feature of the plan is to have one National University Board, meeting at the various associated or affiliated Colleges, which, while retaining their individuality and present independence, will agree to have the course of instruction and the graduation examination regulated by the general University Board—each College or University being equally represented in this Board—to be called the University of Upper Canada. A guarantee will thus be given that the standard of education will be maintained in each College at a proper level, and that no degree shall be conferred except on such students as pass the examination of the examiners of this General Board. It is but just to mention that the University of Toronto, while candidly acknowledging the defects of the present system, has, without a dissenting voice, approved of this plan of securing to Canada a truly National University. The various religious bodies are at present represented in the Senate of the University of Toronto, and their representatives have given a hearty concurrence. We have thus the institutions and parties, hitherto opposed, now as one as to the right constitution of a national University, not confined in its operations to one locality, but embracing the whole province. There is every ground to hope that this unanimity will speedily lead to legislation which will effect a satisfactory and permanent adjustment, and thus gratify the national ambition to have one great National University, which may stand on a level with the older Universities of Europe."

Such is a brief statement of the operations of Queen's College during the twentieth year of her existence. In older and more settled countries Colleges may remain for years without apparent growth, and yet at the same time be efficiently fulfilling their appointed duties. The circumstances and rapid growth of Canada, however, demand equally rapid extension on the part of the Institution of whose interests the Trustees are appointed guardians; and they trust that their yearly Reports may show that Queen's College is keeping pace with the wants of the Province. For sympathy and support the Trustees must look in an especial manner to the venerable Synod about to assemble, and also to the Church which that Court so fully represents. That Queen's College, and more especially her Theological Department, may receive favorable attention, is the earnest request of the Board; but they would respectfully add the hope that the members of Synod will bear the interests of the Institution in mind while laboring in their various spheres of usefulness, and more especially that they will commend its educational advantages to parents and youth with whom they may come in contact. Such influences are invaluable in attracting Students to the College Halls, and by their individual exertions, thus exerted under the Divine blessing, may the Ministers and members of the Church aid in the great work of securing a large and well-trained Ministry to build up and extend that Church throughout the Province.

W. IRELAND,

Secretary to Board of Trustees.

QUEEN'S COLLEGE, }
Kingston, April, 1862. }

	$	c.	$	c.
Royal Charter			3107	37
Apparatus	3562	92		
Library	3187	98		
Furniture, &c.	1380	23		
			8131	13
Bank Stock, 320 shares Commercial Bank	32000	00		
Bonds and Mortgages, viz.:				
A. J. Macdonell (3) $4586	55			
Rice Lewis (5) 4800	00			
A. Mitchell 100	00			
A. Caldwell 400	00			
D. McMillan 150	00			
			10036	55
Lands, viz.:				
16½ acres, Kingston. @ $800... ... ...$13200	00			
100 " S. ½ lot 25, 2nd con. Manvers ... 300	00			
100 " N. ½ " 19, 12th " Portland ... 300	00			
64 " rear " 4, 4th " S. Crosby ... 192	00			
100 " N. ½ " 19, 2nd " Marmora ... 300	00			
100 " E. ½ " 21, 11th " Belmont ... 300	00			
100 " N. ½ " 10, 9th " Tiny ... 300	00			
200 " " 12, 15th " Orillia, N.D., 600	00			
100 " S.E.½ " 10, 12th " Sunnidale ... 300	00			
200 " " 15, 10th " " ... 600	00			
100 " E. ½ " 11, 1st " Plympton ... 300	00			
Lot 4, S. side Hannah street, Hamilton ... 100	00			
			16792	00
College buildings and grounds	35461	39		
Queen's College School and lot	1149	54		
			95439	48
Toronto Scholarship Investment Stock	785	20		
Kingston do. do. do.	1113	00		
			1898	20
Medical Faculty			156	73
Observatory			645	26
Commercial Bank of Canada, viz.:				
Bursary account, contra ... ... $ 405	35			
Prince of Wales endowment... 800	00			
J. Mowat, " 800	00			
Mortgage moneys for re-investment... ... 3272	00			
Available for general purposes 1410	63			
			6687	98
Cash in hands of Treasurer			4	24
			6692	22
			$116070	39

COLLEGE, 9th APRIL, 1862.

					$	c.	$	e.
Toronto Scholarship endowment	...	...	...		800	00		
Kingston do. do.	...	...	...		1113	00		
Prince of Wales do. do.	...	...	...		800	00		
J. Mowat do. do.	...	...	...		800	00		
							3513	00
Bursary account ...	...	...	...	...	...		405	35
Profit and Loss account ...	...	...	...	...			108269	51
Principal Leitch ...	...	...	...	...	2329	14		
Professor Williamson	...	...	...	...	350	00		
Professor Mowat ...	...	...	...	...	375	00		
Professor Weir ...	...	...	...	...	375	00		
Professor Lawson...	...	...	...	...	270	61		
Librarian	...	...	...	...	80	00		
Assistant Teacher Queen's College School	...	...		75	00		
W. Ferguson & Co.'s account	...	...	...		15	17		
G. S. Hobart's do.	...	...	...	...	6	86		
W. Hay's do.	...	...	...	...	4	50		
E. Hamel's do,	...	...	...	...	1	25		
							3882	53

$116070 39

ANDREW DRUMMOND,
April 9, 1862.   Treasurer Q.C.
April 12, 1862—Accounts and vouchers audited and found correct.
GEO. DAVIDS

Dr.   **ABSTRACT STATEMENT, SHOWING RECEIPTS AND**

			$	c.	$	c.
Balance on hand, 9th April, 1861, in Commercial Bank, per statement of that date					4821	38
To special receipts, viz.:						
Account Mortgages			2372	00		
" Medical Faculty			1541	00		
" Bursary account			1017	83		
" Debenture			100	00		
" Observatory			1000	00		
					6030	83
To ordinary receipts, viz.:						
Government grant...			5000	00		
Clergy Reserve Fund			2000	00		
Colonial Committee, Church of Scotland			1426	67		
Interest, dividends, &c.			3742	29		
Fees, matriculation and class			725	58		
					12894	54

$23746 75

13

DISBURSEMENTS, 9th APRIL, 1861, TO 9th APRIL, 1862. Cʀ.

	$ c.	$ c.
By unpaid balances of private accounts, per statement of 9th April, 1861, since paid		3211 25
By special disbursements, viz.:		
Investment Caldwell's mortgage...	1200 00	
Account College buildings and grounds	640 66	
" Travelling expenses, non-resident Trustees ...	100 00	
" Returned fees, Students for Ministry... ...	63 00	
" Prizes, 1860-61	182 63	
" Bursaries to date, per separate account ...	912 00	
" Medical Faculty, do.	1797 01	
" Observatory do.	1645 26	
By ordinary disbursements, viz.:		6540 56

Principal, 12 months to 1st October, 1862 ...$2400 00
Professors Williamson, Weir, and Mowat, 12
   months to 1st October, 1862 ... ... 4500 00
Professor George, 6 months to 1st April, 1862 750 00
Professor Lawson, 12 months to 1st Oct., 1862 1100 00
Secretary to 1st March, 1862... ... ... 150 00
Librarian, Winter Session 1860-61 ... ... 60 00
  Do. one year to 1st May 80 00
Assistant Teacher Queen's College School ... 300 00
Janitors to 1st April 291 67

                          $9631 67
Less proportion Chemical Chair charged
   Medical Faculty above 500 00

	$ c.	$ c.
		9131 67
Advertising, Printing account, Stationery, &c... ...		533 36
Miscellaneous expenses, viz.:		
Fuel and light $161 92		
Sundry accounts for maintenance of property, 226 74		
		388 66
Paid for Postages $25 77, Taxes $6 62...		32 39
" Museum $12 25, Insurance $247 75		260 00
" Prizes, 1861-62		182 63
" Apparatus		109 82
" Books		475 72
" Furniture		71 00
		11185 25
		$20937 06
Deduct amount of unpaid private accounts, per General Statement this date		3882 53
		$17054 53
Balance per General Statement, viz.:		
Commercial Bank deposited	6687 98	
Cash in hands of Treasurer	4 24	
		6692 22
		$23746 75

ANDREW DRUMMOND,

DR. **COMMERCIAL BANK OF CANADA.**

1861.			$	c.
April 9,	To balance	...	4821	38
"	Bursary, St. Andrew's Church, Quebec,	...	50	00
19, "	Instalment on J. Gray's Mortgage	...	121	06
May 1, "	Bursary proc. draft on A. Morris	...	67	75
16, "	Colonial Committee Church of Scotland, £350 stg.	...	1664	45
30, "	Bursary, Seymour Congregation	...	10	00
"	" Martintown "	...	3	00
June 4, "	Government Grant	...	5000	00
6, "	Fees, Prof. Williamson...	...	136	00
8, "	Government Grant, Medical Faculty...	...	1000	00
"	" " Kingston Observatory	...	1000	00
July 2, "	Clergy Reserve Grant ...	...	1000	00
"	Dividend Bank Stock	...	1280	00
"	" Toronto Bursary Stock	...	28	00
"	" Kingston "	...	40	00
24, "	Aberdeen Missionary Association £7...	...	33	60
"	Leeds and Grenville Debenture	...	103	00
Septr. 2, "	Pasture, rent of ...	...	20	00
12, "	A. Mitchell, Bond	...	124	00
17, "	A. Caldwell, prepayment on Mortgage due 25th March next	...	140	00

1861.	By Cheques, viz :		$	c.
April 11, 615,	Observatory		20	50
13, 616,	J K. McMorine		47	00
13, 617,	A. McLennan...		16	00
13, 618,	Caldwell's Mortgage		1165	13
23, 619,	Ten Bursaries...		240	00
620,	Seven "		160	00
621,	One "		36	00
622,	J. C. Smith		60	00
30, 623,	Three Bursaries		100	00
624,	Principal Leitch		352	31
May 1, 625,	do. Mrs. Vardon		8	00
626,	G. W. Draper...		30	00
627,	Wilson and Sons acct. Principal		15	62
2, 628,	Postmaster do.		12	41
4, 629,	W. Darrach		60	00
11, 630,	F. F. Harkness		40	00
16, 631,	E. J. Barker		18	40
17, 632,	J. Rowlands		38	98
633,	Armstrong & Benedict		15	00
634,	A. Watson		20	00
18, 635,	J. M. Creighton		139	00
636,	Prof. George		450	00
637,	J. Rowlands		21	52
22, 638,	Davidson, Bruce & Doran		18	15
23, 639,	Mrs. Gill		24	00
June 5, 640,	Prof. Williamson		375	00
641,	Prof. Yates, ...		15	00
8, 642,	J. Peabody		13	40
643,	E. J. Barker		3	00
10, 644,	John Paton		26	32
645,	W. Darrach		30	00
13, 646,	S. Anglin		4	08
15, 647,	J. M. Creighton		116	85
648,	Dr. Lawson		2	50
649,	Do.		100	00
28, 650,	W. Darrach		36	49
July 3, 651,	Prof. George		375	00
4, 652,	F. F. Harkness		36	00
5, 653,	Prof. Weir		344	25
6, 654,	J. B. May		75	00
11, 655,	Royal Insurance Company		37	50
15, 656,	T. W. Robison		47	07
18, 657,	J. M. Creighton		39	75
19, 658,	W. Allen		6	00
29, 659,	Joseph Bruce...		27	22
Aug. 2, 660,	Prof. Mowat		375	00
8, 661,	Prof. Lawson		90	00
10, 662,	J. Cormack		30	00
663,	Do.		7	13
664,	E. J. Barker		5	00
24, 665,	Prof. Williamson		40	00

Dʀ. **COMMERCIAL BANK OF CANADA.**

			$	c.
1861.				
	Brought forward	...16642	24
Octr. 9,	To Fees, Prof. Lawson	28	00
Novr. 8,	" N. Borden's Mortgage	106	00
8,	" Rice Lewis' "	144	00
Decr. 7,	" Prepayment on Caldwell's Mortgage, due March next	240	00
1862.				
Jany. 3,	" Bursary, J. Watkins, Esq.	60	00
4,	" Fees, Prof. Weir...	80	00
7,	" A. Pentland, Mortgage...	540	00
	" Dividend, Bank Stock	1280	00
	" " Bursary "	28	00
	" " " "	40	00
	" Interest on account current	291	86
11,	" Clergy Reserve Grant	1000	00
18,	" Cheque 711, Dr. Barclay, cancelled	22	00
21,	" Prepayment from A. Caldwell on Mortgage	164	00
29,	" Bursary, St. Andrew's Church, Perth	24	00

COMMERCIAL BANK OF CANADA.   Cr.

1861.	Brought forward						...$5365 58
Aug. 31,	666, W. Ireland						6 92
	667, Do.						50 00
	668, J. Cormack						17 90
Sept. 12,	669, P. Web...						30 00
13,	670, J. Milne						99 00
21,	671, J. Tossell						200 00
	672, J. Cormack						15 50
22,	673, Chown & Cunningham						4 17
	674, Do.						8 00
	675, J. Cormack						45 00
25,	676, Rev. A. Spence						6 20
Octr. 1,	677, Prof. Williamson						713 12
	678, Prof. Lawson ...						550 00
	679, Prof. Mowat ...						750 00
	680, Prof. Weir						750 00
2,	681, J. M. Creighton						13 50
4,	682, R. Irving						150 00
8,	683, Prof. George ...						400 00
	684, Jno. May						75 00
9,	685, Prof. Lawson ...						10 20
10,	686, J. Cormack						34 08
	687, R. Irving						100 00
	688, R. Tossell						100 00
Novr. 1,	689, P. Ferguson ...						6 62
2,	690, W. Irving & Son						34 09
	691, Robert Irving...						150 00
	692, R. Tossell						100 00
9,	693, Liverpool and London Insurance Company						30 00
	694, S. Muckleston...						83 01
	695, Royal Insurance Company ...						5 25
19,	696, James Morton...						20 65
20,	697, J. Cormack						40 00
22,	698, Express Company						5 41
	699, W. Anglin						67 93
25,	700, R. Irving						140 00
29,	701, R. Tossell						283 70
	702, Andrew Davidson						200 00
Decr. 2,	703, W. Ireland						53 77
4,	704, J. M. Creighton						12 00
5,	705, Royal Insurance Company ...						25 00
	706, Mrs. Gill						2 50
12,	707, Rev. Dr. Urquhart						5 50
13,	708, Rev. Duncan Morrison						8 00
17,	709, Luhme & Co ...						62 72
19,	710, J. Cameron						22 00
19,	711, Rev. Dr. Barclay (cancelled and cred. contra)						22 00
	712, Rev. A. Spence						10 50
20,	713, Rev. Dr. Cook...						20 00
21,	714, J. May...						75 00
	715, R. Irving						142 75
	716, J. Paton						9 57

DR.   **COMMERCIAL BANK OF CANADA.**

1862.							$	c.
	Brought forward	...	...	...	...	...	...20690	10
Feb. 12,	To Bursary, Kingston Congregation	...	...	...	...	41	00
14,	" " J. Watkins, Esq.,	...	...	...	...	80	00
14,	" " Guelph Congregation...	...	...	...	22	00
21,	" " Ottawa "	...	...	...	30	00
	" " additional Kingston Congregation	...	...	4	00
Mch. 4,	" Fees, Prof. George	...	...	...	...	64	05
5,	" Bursary, Fergus Congregation ...	...	...	...	10	65
	" " Hamilton "	...	...	...	...	44	05
	" " Cornwall "	...	...	...	...	40	00
	" " Valcartier "	...	...	...	...	3	00
13,	" Rice Lewis, interest	...	...	...	...	144	00
25,	" Sir H. Smith, mortgage ...	...	...	...	...	928	30
April 1,	" Caldwell do.	...	...	...	...	256	00
1,	" Interest do.	...	...	...	...	61	20
3,	" H. Allan, Bursary,	...	...	...	...	50	00
4,	" Fees, Prof. Weir ...	...	...	...	...	72	00
4,	" Balance Matriculation fees	...	...	...	184	89

$22725 19

1862.
April 9, To balance $6687 98

COMMERCIAL BANK OF CANADA. Cr.

	Brought forward	$11132	14
Decr. 24,	717, Prof. Williamson	99	45
	718, do.	11	75
24,	719, J. Cormack	3	06
30,	720, Prof. Lawson	36	00
1862.			
Jany. 3,	721, J. Cormack	36	28
4,	722, Prof. George	350	00
7,	723, Phœnix Insurance Company	30	00
8,	724, Principal Leitch	1000	00
	725, G. Brown	42	58
11,	726, A. Davidson	191	32
18,	727, Rev. Dr. Barclay	13	80
25,	728, J. Kinnear	20	50
Feby. 3,	729, Bursaries	140	00
8,	730, J. Duff...	51	00
	731, Bursaries	100	00
12,	732, Rev. J. McMorine	4	00
	733, R. M. Horsey...	14	15
15,	734, A. Newlands	55	82
17,	735, J. Cormack	35	00
18,	736, Bursary	20	00
19,	737, J. Smith	47	25
20,	738, Chown & Cunningham	1	67
21,	739, T. W. Robison	81	88
25,	740, H. Skinner	39	89
	741, S. T. Drennan...	36	00
	742, Bursary	20	00
March 1,	743, W. Ireland	53	79
3,	744, W. C. Chewett & Co....	64	50
5,	745, Royal Insurance Company	120	00
13,	746, Rev. J. McMorine	4	00
15,	747, W. Irving & Son	11	70
	748, do.	9	70
20,	749, Rev. Dr. Urquhart	6	00
April 1,	750, Prof. Mowat	375	00
	751, Prof. Williamson	400	00
	752, Prof. Lawson	250	00
4,	753, Prof. Weir	375	00
5,	754, Fraser & George	16	34
	755, J. Cormack	41	25
7,	756, Paton & Ritchie	189	44
	757, A. Adie & Son	116	69
	758, Murray & Son...	365	26
	759, B. Dawson & Son	25	00
	Balance	6687	98
		$22725	19

ANDREW DRUMMOND,

Treasurer Q.C,

DR. PETTY CASH ACCOUNT.

			$	c.
1861.				
May 20,	To J. Rowlands, error in account		2	30
21,	" Seymour Congregation, for Bursary		10	00
June 15,	" Belleville Congregation, do.		5	00
1862.				
Feb. 17,	" Additional Kingston do. do.		4	00
March 4,	" Fergus do. do.		10	65
26,	" Orangeville do. do.		2	00

$33 95

April 9, Balance on hand ... ... $4 24.

Lightning Source UK Ltd.
Milton Keynes UK
UKHW012158150219
337363UK00004B/199/P